HSA
OWNER'S MANUAL

HSA

OWNER'S MANUAL
SECOND EDITION

What Every Accountholder, Employer and
Benefits Consultant Needs to
Know about Health Savings Accounts –
and How to Use Them Strategically

Todd Berkley

Published in the United States of America

ISBN: 978-0-69287-290-1
1. Business & Economics / Insurance / Health
2. Reference / Handbooks & Manuals
15.09.04

ACKNOWLEDGMENTS

I'd like to thank my Dad for encouraging my passion for education and business. He published a daily paper for many years, I hope my book will make him proud. I'd also like to thank my wife, Kelly, and my family for their love and support and for enduring my passion for all things HSA. I am indebted to my colleagues throughout the HSA industry who dedicate themselves to helping people understand, embrace, and benefit from the differences a Health Savings Account can bring to the health care and retirement planning experience.

I'd also like to thank Ewell Brown for his assistance with the organization of the topics in the book. And a big thank-you to Cynthia M., my top-notch editor, who made the text more consistent and readable.

Please note that I am not a lawyer. This book does not represent legal advice. Instead, I merely attempt to distill extraordinarily complex information that may prevent you from choosing an HSA-qualified plan (or paralyze your decision making if your employer has made the plan choice for you) and present it in easy-to-understand portions. I have included references to original sources where practical. I encourage you to share this information with your personal tax advisor to make sure that you comply with all IRS rules and regulations governing HSAs.

CONTENTS

Part 3

HSA Strategies

Part 4

Appendices

FOREWORD

This book is the owner's manual that did not come with your HSA.

Health Savings Accounts are becoming a more common part of average Americans' lives. Paired with HSA-qualified health plans, they cover a growing number of Americans' health care costs. And the trends indicate that they'll become an even more important part of more people's health care in the future.

This book is designed to help you understand HSAs and HSA-qualified health plans. When you enroll in these plans, you often receive a mass of literature about the health plan, outlining what services are covered, your cost-sharing, exclusions, rules to follow, and how to appeal a claim denial, among other topics. You probably received some information about the HSA itself from your trustee. It most likely came in the form of a glossy twelve-page brochure with pictures of smiling families and caring doctors, plus some very basic information about how to set up your account, how much you could contribute, and a partial list of expenses eligible for tax-free distribution.

That level of information is simply inadequate for you to manage your HSA. If you rely on that information alone, you'll probably end up doing something inadvertently that runs afoul of HSA rules and regulations. Even if your HSA custodian is the rare one that provides adequate and easy-to-understand information in its printed materials and online to keep you in compliance, you'll never learn how to maximize the benefit of your HSA. HSA trustees simply do not provide this information.

So where do you turn for complete information on remaining compliant with HSA rules and regulations *and* maximizing the short-term and long-term tax advantages of your HSA? Right here, with this book. *HSA Owner's Manual* is the most comprehensive guide to HSAs available anywhere. *This book is the owner's manual that did not come with your HSA.* If you follow the advice in this book, you'll keep your HSA in compliance with current HSA rules and regulations. You'll also learn about sources of updated information as the IRS releases new rules and interpretations and as the Department of Health and Human Services issues health care reform regulations that impact HSAs.

Your HSA trustee may offer similar information, but probably not in an easy-to-understand format and certainly not in a single volume.

In addition, **this book delivers information that no HSA trustee offers—strategies to help you maximize your financial opportunity** as an HSA accountholder. You'll learn how to integrate your HSA into your short-term tax savings and long-term asset building strategies. You'll receive information that will help you determine when you should use your HSA as a reimbursement account and when you'll benefit from utilizing it as a long-term financial asset.

May your journey through the pages of this book reduce your confusion about your HSA and help you embrace it to unlock its hidden value for your long-term financial health.

> If you would like to receive updates as HSA rules change, please visit or subscribe to AskMrHSA.com, an educational service run by my company, HSA Consulting Services, LLC.

HOW THIS BOOK
IS ORGANIZED

This book contains four sections.

Part 1: You'll learn about the "rules of engagement" that govern HSAs. Each chapter gathers the rules associated with one broad topic, like *Eligibility*, *Contributions* and *Distributions*. If you have a question about a specific topic, you can review that chapter and find a brief discussion of that specific topic. In many cases, you'll also see a reference to the original legislation or an IRS interpretation that will guide you further in your understanding of the topic.

Part 2: This section contains much of the information included in Section 1, but it arranges that information by specific situations. For example, if you are wondering how Medicare impacts your HSA, you can turn to the "HSAs and Medicare" chapter and find a discussion of the eligibility, contribution, and distribution rules specific to Medicare.

Part 3: In this section, you'll learn about specific strategies that you can adopt to get the most out of your HSA. You'll need to read Section 1 first, since these strategies will not make sense without a solid foundation in HSA "rules of engagement."

Part 4:   This section contains original source reference material. You may want to refer to it to gain additional knowledge about a very specific topic.

How to Read This Book

Authors of novels do not have to instruct readers on how to read their books. You know to start at the beginning and read through to the end. If you read it any other way, you'll miss too much, and the ending will not make sense.

Reference books like *HSA Owner's Manual* are different. They do not read like a novel. So here's the best way to read this book:

- **Read Part 1 first.** You need to understand the basic "rules of engagement" that apply to HSAs. Without this foundation, you cannot manage your HSA successfully. Regardless of your personal situation, most of the information in Section 1 applies to you.
- **Read specific topics in Part 2 that apply to your personal situation.** Part 2 summarizes the key points based on personal situations, rather than delivering information by broad topic. For example, if you are divorced, you need to understand the specific rules around HSA eligibility, contributions, and distributions for individuals who are divorced. These topics are included in the *Eligibility*, *Contributions*, and *Distributions* sections, but they are scattered among topical sections. Part 2 brings all the information related to personal situations into one place.
- **Glance at Part 3 when you open your HSA.** You may find a topic relevant when you first open your HSA (for

example, Strategies 1, 2, and 3 may be relevant to you immediately). Read in depth the particular strategies that immediately make sense to you.

- **Read Part 3 in depth within a year.** Once you begin to manage your HSA and become comfortable with making deposits, identifying and reimbursing eligible expenses, understanding what expenses are subject to the deductible under your HSA-qualified plan, and matching up insurance statements (often called Explanations of Benefits) with provider bills, you'll be ready to absorb higher-level information. At that point, you may find a strategy that will help you manage your HSA more effectively or maximize your tax savings or build your wealth faster.
- **Read Part 4 as appropriate.** It contains some original sources such as the full text of Section 223 of the Internal Revenue Code (IRC), the HSA law, plus a list of other resources. You'll want to consult the online resources at times to receive the most up-to-date information on HSAs.

The keys to your success in managing your HSA are your willingness to learn, the principles presented in this book, and your patience and discipline as you strive to understand a program that may seem very confusing at first.

If you are totally frustrated after three months, remain patient. If you are still totally frustrated after six months, remain patient. If you are committed to understanding how HSAs work and how your health plan and HSA can work for you, you'll get it. In my experience, most people are dragged into HSAs against their will ("Why don't I get to keep my Cadillac plan?"), but over time, the overwhelming majority of folks learn to love it. Your understanding may be gradual, or you may be totally confused one day and find that everything clicks the next day. In the end, you'll master the information that you need to manage your HSA and integrate it into your personal financial plan.

The author is not a lawyer, and this book does not constitute legal advice. You must consult your own personal legal or tax advisor to receive counsel appropriate to your situation. Also, as the IRS periodically issues new guidance, Congress passes legislation and tax courts interpret the law, the information in this book may no longer be correct at the time that you read and apply it. That's another reason why it is important to receive good, timely advice from your personal legal or tax advisor.

INTRODUCTION

An important revolution is taking place in health care.

You may already be participating. If not, you almost certainly will be during the next five years, whether you continue to buy insurance through your employer or move to individual coverage on your own.

The front lines in this revolution include those who signed up voluntarily and those who were conscripted. It does not matter how you arrived or whether you've arrived yet. Your time is coming. You may fight it, but when you embrace it, you will find it changes the lens with which you view your current and future health care interactions.

The revolution is the Health Savings Account (HSA) program. Actually, it is two programs in one. First, there's an HSA-qualified health plan, which includes a broad up-front deductible. In this sense, it is similar to traditional insurance lines like homeowner's, renter's, and automobile insurance. An HSA-qualified plan provides comprehensive health coverage, but only after the policyholder pays the cost of services before reaching the dollar figure at which insurance begins to reimburse expenses.

Second, there's a Health Savings Account, a tax-advantaged vehicle that allows eligible individuals to divert a portion of their income or assets from the taxable income stream and set the funds aside in an account from which they can reimburse eligible expenses tax-free and efficiently save for future health care expenses.

The two plans essentially work in unison. An individual cannot have an HSA account without enrolling in the HSA-qualified health plan (and meeting certain other eligibility criteria). An individual enrolled on an HSA-qualified health plan does not have to open and contribute to an HSA, but failure to do so results in a lost financial opportunity.

Because the health plan includes a broad deductible, its premium is generally lower than more traditional health insurance plans that have lower cost sharing. Insurers price the product lower for two reasons. First, the policyholder shares more of the up-front costs that the insurer otherwise would reimburse. Second, the insurer factors in a change of behavior that naturally occurs when a policyholder bears more of the cost of services. Since, as the late Nobel laureate Milton Friedman astutely observed, "[v]ery few people spend other people's money as carefully as they spend their own," insurers reason that policyholders who are responsible for up-front costs, and can bank the savings, are more likely to spend their money prudently, which impacts utilization of the healthcare system.

While the pain of moderate out-of-pocket expenses is felt directly by the insured party, once the underlying insurance kicks in, it provides substantial security again catastrophic loss. In fact, an HSA-qualified policy is the only type of health insurance that always has a maximum out-of-pocket limit by law. The HSA-style maximum limits will soon be adopted by all insurance policies sold as the Affordable Care Act rolls out and initial waivers expire.

The program is designed to introduce deductibles (or higher deductibles) without diluting the value of insurance, whether the policyholder purchases insurance through his employer or in the individual market. Let's look at the economics in the employer-based insurance scenario, assuming a health plan with a $4,000 deductible and a savings of $3,000 in premium, split in a 1:2 ratio between employee ($1,000 saved) and employer ($2,000 saved). The employee directs his $1,000 pre-tax into his HSA, and the employer contributes 80% of its savings into the employee's HSA. The employee has covered $2,600 of his $4,000 deductible in the form of deposits to his HSA account.

For many employees, $2,600 will more than cover their deductible expenses for the year. In other cases, they'll need to make additional contributions, which they can make on a pre-tax or after-tax basis. An employee who contributes an additional $1,400 to cover his entire deductible will generate tax savings of about $500, leaving him $900 worse off (covering only $3,100 of his deductible before he begins to feel the financial impact). The same individual who contributes an additional $4,050 (up to the $6,750 maximum HSA contribution in 2014) saves about $1,700 in taxes, effectively reaching a break-even point even if he incurs his entire $4,000 deductible.

The math is important. Moving to a higher deductible does not constitute a reduction in the value of employer-based insurance. Instead, it is often a rational change instituted by the employer that results in overall savings for most employees. In fact, studies show that when individuals purchase insurance in the individual market or on a health insurance exchange, they consistently choose a combination of lower premiums and higher deductibles than their former employer-based plan. And when employers offer two or more plans with fixed-dollar contributions (the employer pays the same amount of each policy's premium, so that the employee who wants to buy the plan with a lower deductible pays the entire premium difference between the two plans), employees consistently choose lower premiums and higher deductibles.

Thus, the introduction of an HSA-qualified plan with an up-front deductible does not reduce the value of insurance. Rather, the program rearranges the same dollars in a way that gives individuals an incentive to be more prudent in their purchases and rewards them (by allowing them to retain funds that they'd otherwise spend on premiums and deposit those funds into a tax-advantaged account) by reducing their taxable income. Put another way, there is a 100% chance you will pay a premium, but only some chance that you will pay out-of-pocket costs. It is often smart to take some risk of potentially higher out-of-pocket cost for a sure reduction of premium going to the insurance company.

HSA programs have broad appeal once consumers understand how they work. When HSAs were introduced in 2004, critics scoffed that they benefitted only the "healthy, wealthy and wise," while leaving lower-income, higher utilizing and less sophisticated individuals worse off. The experience of the last ten years has not borne out this criticism.

In fact, many policyholders pay less in total out-of-pocket costs (premium and cost-sharing) than they did under their old health plan with higher premiums and lower out-of-pocket costs. For many, HSAs are the alternative to the tax-advantaged Health Flexible Spending Arrangements (Health FSAs) to which they did not have access because either their employer could not afford the administrative costs or they were business owners who were not eligible to participate. But unlike FSAs, they do not need to accurately predict out of pocket costs for the year and be pressured to spend everything in the calendar year.

For others, the lower premium has "reset the premium baseline," allowing their employer to continue to offer employer-based insurance at premiums that both employer and employee can afford. For many lower-income accountholders, the money their employer deposits into their HSA account is very empowering; it is often the first time they have ever owned a savings account. And for those with lower utilization due to youth, sheer luck, or adoption of a healthy lifestyle, HSAs represent an opportunity to build a financial asset and save for future heath care costs in retirement.

This book is not written to make the case for HSAs, to evaluate whether they are the best insurance option for an individual or employee population, or to evaluate employer program design and implementation strategies. Instead, it is written for individuals (and in the case of employer-based insurance, employers and brokers or benefit consultants) who are already covered by an HSA-qualified health plan and want to make the most of it. The goal of this book is to provide comprehensive information for HSA accountholders so that they can use the flexibility written into the HSA legislation to apply the program in a way that makes the most financial sense for them.

The most basic confusion I encounter when answering questions for people at AskMrHSA.com is mixing up the rules between making a tax-free contribution to an account and how you can use the money once it is in the HSA account. There is actually a strong dividing line between the two. There is a very rigid set of rules regarding which individuals can open and contribute to an HSA and how much they can deposit each year. *HSA contribution eligibility is all about carrying the right insurance coverage at the right time*.

Once the money is placed into the HSA, the rules shift dramatically. Now coverage does not matter. *Using your HSA to pay for medical expenses tax-free is all about paying the right expenses at the right time for people who are related to you in the right way*, either through marriage or through your tax return.

Most of this book is devoted to helping you sort out these basic rules but also to move beyond them to take advantage of the powerful set of options those simple rules open up to you. You may not have asked for an HSA plan and may have even hated the idea at first, but my hope is that, now that you are here, this book will help you make the most of the current situation and even help you embrace your HSA to see the worlds of health care and financial planning in a whole new light.

GLOSSARY

I have tried to avoid health and banking industry jargon as much as possible in this owner's manual, but some of it is unavoidable. The following are plain English definitions of some of the industry terms used in this manual:

Health Savings Account (HSA)—An individually owned trust account that provides tax-free savings for qualified medical expenses.

HSA Qualified Plan—A high-deductible health plan that serves as the base qualification for individuals to contribute to an HSA. The IRS sets parameters for the qualifying plan that change yearly with inflation.

HSA Eligible Individual—A person who is currently covered by an HSA-qualified plan, not a dependent on someone else's tax return and not disqualified by other health coverage—these factors allow him to contribute to an HSA.

HSA Contribution Limit—The maximum amount an HSA accountholder can contribute to his or her HSA each calendar year. The IRS publishes annual limits adjusted for inflation.

HSA Tax-Free Eligible Medical Expenses—Expenses that meet requirements of IRS section 213-d to diagnose or treat an illness, injury, or condition that are eligible for tax-free reimbursement from an HSA or other healthcare spending account.

HSA Trustee (or Custodian or Administrator)—The company approved by the IRS to offer trusts known as HSAs. Usually a bank or investment firm, but other companies my be approved by the IRS to offer HSAs.

HSA Transfer or Rollover—Money moving from one HSA to another owned by the same individual. Transfers move directly between trustees; rollovers are withdrawn by the accountholder and deposited into the new HSA within 60 days.

IRA Transfer or Rollover to HSA—The ability to move money from an IRA or Roth IRA to an HSA once in a lifetime. These transfers reduce that year's HSA contribution limit. IRA transfers happen directly between the IRA Trustee and the HSA trustee; rollovers are withdrawn by the accountholder and deposited to the HSA within 60 days.

Health Plan Deductible—The amount of money the insured individual must pay toward medical expenses before insurance covers kicks in. HSA qualified plans have minimum deductible published each year by the IRS for all covered expenses except preventive care.

Health Plan Out of Pocket Maximum (OOP)—The total amount you could pay out of pocket in any given year, including the deductible, co-pays, and coinsurance after which the insurance company pays 100%.

Health Plan Co-Pay—A fixed payment paid before insurance will pay for each service at the health providers office such as $20 for each doctor visit or each prescription.

Health Plan Coinsurance—A percentage of each medical expense shared by the insurance company and the family or individual, typically 80% paid by insurance company and 20% co-insurance paid by the insured person.

Flexible Spending Account (FSA)—an employer-sponsored program that allows employees to choose to receive a portion of their pay in the form of pre-tax contributions to an account out of which they can draw funds tax-free to pay for certain health-related expenses. Funds must be used each year or forfeited back to the employer. Health FSAs are not compatible with HSAs.

Limited-Purpose Flexible Spending Account (LPFSA)—an employer-sponsored program that allows employees to choose to receive a portion of their pay in the form of pre-tax contributions to an account out of which they can draw funds tax-free to pay for health-related expenses limited to dental and vision. Funds must be used each year or forfeited back to the employer. LPFSAs are compatible with HSAs.

FSA Rollover—A new provision that allows an FSA participant to extend up to $500 of remaining funds into the next plan year. Allows participant to convert rollover to an HSA-compatible LPFSA, if employer plan allows.

FSA Grace Period—An extended period of three and one-half months to utilize remaining FSA funds at the end of a plan year. The grace period is incompatible with an HSA and means affected participants are not HSA-eligible until the beginning of the fourth month.

Health Spending Arrangement (HRA)—an employer-sponsored program that pairs a high deductible health plan with an employer funded account out of which they can draw funds tax-free to pay for certain health-related expenses. HRAs are not compatible with HSAs.

Post-Deductible FSA or HRA—an employer-sponsored program that allows employees to choose to receive a portion of their pay in the form of pre-tax contributions to an account out of which they can draw funds tax-free to pay for health-related expenses only after a minimum deductible is met on the HSA qualified plan. Post-deductible accounts are compatible with HSAs.

PART 1
HSA RULES

HSA-QUALIFIED PLAN

This is the one chapter of this book that focuses solely on the underlying health plan. It is an important part of the HSA program, and you need to understand what constitutes an HSA-qualified plan and how the plan works.

You must be enrolled in an HSA-qualified plan (referred to in the law as a High Deductible Health Plan) to become HSA-eligible. A qualified plan typically will have "HSA" as part of its name, but not always. Be sure that your plan is HSA-qualified. Many high deductible plans look like HSA-qualified plans at first glance (for example, they meet the minimum deductible stated below), but the deductible does not cover a broad enough range of services or the family deductible does not work as qualified plan rules require. Your insurance company will usually make it clear whether or not a plan is HSA-qualified, but if you are not sure whether the plan is qualified, you should check with the insurance regulator in your state. *IRC Section 223(c)(1)(A) and IRS Notice 2004-2.*

All covered services except select preventive care are subject to a deductible. The list of services subject to the deductible (the amount the insured person must pay at 100% before insurance coverage kicks in) includes diagnostic office visits, diagnostic testing and imaging, treatments and prescription drugs. This list is far broader than many standard deductible plans, which subject diagnostics and treatment to the deductible but cover prescription drugs, physician office visits, and sometimes other types of visits (such as chiropractic care, outpatient therapy, and home health) subject to a copay (a flat fee paid regardless of the service provided) rather than the deductible. Under an HSA-qualified plan, all these encounters with health care practitioners and all prescription drugs are subject to a deductible. *IRS Notice 2004-2, Q&A 3.*

Insurers are allowed to cover certain select preventive services at a richer benefit level by removing them from the deductible. Certain preventive services are now covered in full under most health plans sold in the United States as a result of the Patient Protection and Affordable Care Act of 2010 (commonly referred to as the Affordable Care Act, or ACA). Note: Some employers chose to "grandfather" their health plans or may have been granted an exception from ACA standards. Certain provisions of the ACA, including full coverage for certain preventive services, may not apply to grandfathered plans.

Insurers have the option to cover other select preventive services with cost sharing—either subject to a copay or coinsurance (a percent of the remaining bill after the deductible has been satisfied) or included in the medical deductible. For example, an HSA-qualified health plan that covers routine physicals in full per the requirements of the ACA may charge a $25 copay for a routine eye exam or cover the eye exam subject to the deductible. *IRC Section 223(c)(2)(C), IRS Notice 2004-2, Q&A 3* and *IRS Notice 2004-23.*

An HSA-qualified plan must meet the minimum deductible level set by the Internal Revenue Service. This statutory minimum annual deductible is the amount that you must pay for services (other than select preventive services that are covered in full or with cost-sharing outside the deductible) that you (and family members, if you are covered under a family contract) receive within a given twelve-month period of time. The IRS adjusts the figures every spring for the next calendar year to reflect changes in the general Consumer Price Index.

The figures for 2015 and 2016 are the following:

	2015	2016
• Self-only contract:	$1,300	$1,300
• Family contract:	$2,600	$2,600

IRC Section 223(b)(2)(A)(i), Rev. Proc. 2014-30 and Rev. Proc. 2015-30.

A family contract is defined as any policy that covers two or more individuals, regardless of the deductible tiers or rating tiers. The contract is considered a family policy even if it covers only two people and is called a "dual" or "individual plus one" or "individual and spouse" or "individual plus child." Any contract that covers more than one person is subject to the statutory minimum annual deductible for a family contract. *IRC Section 223 (c)(4)* and *IRS Notice 2004-50, Q&A 12.*

If the family contract has a lower deductible for each family member, that individual member deductible cannot be less than the statutory minimum annual deductible for a family contract. Insurers construct their family deductibles in one of two ways.

Under an *aggregate*, or *umbrella*, deductible design, all family members' deductible claims are subject to a single family deductible. Thus, one family member alone can meet the entire deductible, or several or all members together can contribute to meeting the deductible. If the family deductible is $5,000, the insurer does not begin to pay benefits until the family has incurred $5,000 of deductible expenses, regardless of whether one family member or multiple members incur the expenses.

Under an *embedded* deductible, the insurer includes an individual deductible under the family deductible. For example, if the insurer has a $6,000 family deductible with each family member's deductible capped at $3,000, the family faces a lower deductible limit if only one family member incurs deductible expenses.

The rules for an HSA-qualified plan require that if there is an embedded deductible, any individual deductible must be at least as high as the statutory minimum annual deductible for a family contract. A family contract with a $4,000 family deductible that caps each family member's financial responsibility at $2,000 (or any figure less than $2,600 in 2016) is not HSA-qualified, even if it meets all other criteria. *IRS Notice 2004-2, Q&A 3.*

An HSA-qualified plan must cap total out-of-pocket expenses for covered services at an amount not to exceed the statutory maximum out-of-pocket expenses set by the IRS. The statutory annual out-of-pocket maximum represents the highest total out-of-pocket costs for which an individual or family is financially responsible in a given year after which the insurer pays 100% of all covered services. This figure includes copays (fixed dollar amounts, such as a $25 copay for a prescription drug), deductible, and coinsurance (shared responsibility between the patient and insurer, as in the situation in which the insurer pays 80% of a bill, leaving the patient with 20% coinsurance). The IRS reviews this figure annually and adjusts for general inflation. In 2015 and 2016, the figures are the following:

	2015	2016
• Self-only contract:	$6,450	$6,550
• Family contract:	$12,900	$13,100

IRC Section 223(c)(2)(A)(ii), Rev. Proc. 2014-30 and Rev. Proc. 2015-30

An HSA-qualified plan can have out-of-pocket maximums below these statutory maximum figures. Insurers often set members' maximum financial responsibility below the maximum figures for competitive reasons. They do not want their policies to appear to be unattractive relative to other health insurance plans offered in their market. In fact, a well-respected survey tracks this figure each year and in 2014 found that the average

HSA maximum out-of-pocket limit was $3,953 for individual plans and $7,791 for family HSA plans, well below the IRS-mandated maximums. Be sure to read your policy information carefully to determine your maximum out-of-pocket exposure for both in-network (subject to these statutory limits) and out-of-network (not limited by Section 223) benefit levels. *IRS Notice 2004-2, Q&A 3, Kaiser Family Foundation and HRET, "Employer Health Benefits" Annual Survey 2014.*

If your expenses under a self-only contract or a family's expenses under a family contract for covered services reach this maximum, all remaining services are covered in full for the remainder of the year. Meeting the out-of-pocket maximum is a "good news/bad news" proposition. The bad news is that you have a substantial financial responsibility to the healthcare system. The good news is that HSA rules provide a ceiling (often reduced by your health insurer in your policy's plan design) on the maximum financial responsibility that you can incur in a given twelve-month period for covered services. HSA-qualified plans cannot have unlimited member financial responsibility and therefore help people avoid financial calamity that can be caused by large medical bills where the out-of-pocket costs are not capped. *IRC Section 223((c)(2)(A)(ii) and IRS Notice 2004-2, Q&A 3.*

The statutory annual out-of-pocket maximum applies to in-network services only. If the health plan provides coverage for non-contracted providers, the statutory annual out-of-pocket maximum does not apply to those services. HSA-qualified plans are often Preferred Provider Organizations, or PPOs. One distinguishing characteristic of typical PPO plans is that members can receive services from providers not contracted with the health plan, though at a lower level of benefits (often a higher deductible). In these cases, the statutory annual out-of-pocket maximum applies to in-network services only. Under federal HSA rules, your insurer can impose higher out-of-pocket limits (including no out-of-pocket limits, leaving you with unlimited financial responsibility) for those out-of-network services. Your state may impose out-of-pocket maximums on out-of-network expenses. *IRC Section 223 (c)(2)(D) and IRS Notice 2004-2 Q&A 4.*

Prescription drugs are subject to the deductible under an HSA-qualified plan. For many individuals enrolled in an HSA-qualified plan, having prescription drugs subject to the deductible is a major benefit change. Prescription drugs under non-HSA-qualified plans are often covered by copay (you pay a flat dollar amount and never know the real cost of a prescription) or coinsurance (you pay a percentage of the actual cost, so you know the actual cost but are shielded from the full cost by your insurer's covering a large percentage of that cost). Insurers do not have the option of assuming any financial responsibility for prescription drugs before you meet the health plan deductible (but see below for a modification of that situation). Consequently, this is an area where significant behavior and cost control changes occur, as those in HSA plans become more aware of the high cost of brand-name drugs and often switch to lower cost generics. *IRS Notice 2004-2 Q&A 3.*

Insurers are allowed to cover select preventive prescriptions outside the deductible. Under HSA rules, an insurer can offer preventive prescription drugs at a richer benefit level, just as it can for select preventive medical services. Prescription drugs are trickier, though, because there is no clear industry definition of what constitutes a preventive prescription. Insurers initially were slow to offer preventive prescription drugs outside the deductible, but in recent years national carriers and many regional plans have defined a list of preventive prescription drugs that they cover at a richer benefit level. *IRS Notice 2004-50, Q&A 27.*

If an individual is covered by separate medical insurance and prescription drug or behavioral health plans, both/ all plans must be HSA-qualified plans in order for the individual to remain HSA-eligible. Sometimes, large employers assemble components of their employees' health coverage rather than buying a single comprehensive plan that includes all medical benefits. In these cases, employers contract with a prescription drug or behavioral health program, then purchase a health insurance plan that "carves out" that service. You still receive comprehensive care, and you may not even notice the difference as you access care, but you technically have two or more health plans. In this case, for you to be HSA-eligible, one of two things needs to happen. First, the two or three separate components must coordinate with each other to track your deductible, so that no plan begins to pay benefits before you reach the statutory minimum annual deductible. Second, as a less attractive alternative, both/all plans must have separate deductibles that meet the statutory minimum annual deductible ($1,300 for self-only and $2,600 for family contracts in 2016). Under this second scenario, if your employer offers separate health and prescription drug plans and the two plans do not coordinate deductibles, *each* component must have a minimum $2,600 deductible (which could result in up to $5,200 or $7,800 total deductible expenses) for a family contract. *IRS Notice 2004-38.*

If a policy's deductible year is more than twelve months, the statutory minimum annual deductible must be adjusted upward. This situation most likely occurs either as (1) a one-time event during the transition to an HSA-qualified plan or (2) as a regular plan feature, as in a fourth-quarter deductible carryover. As an example of the former, on May 1, 2016, your employer moves from a non-HSA-qualified plan that tracks the deductible on a calendar year to a HSA-qualified plan with a plan-year deductible. If you receive a credit for the deductible that you incurred between January and April 2016, you have, in effect, a sixteen-month deductible year (January 1 through the following April 30). In this case, the minimum deductible must be adjusted to determine whether your plan is qualified.

The minimum deductible for a family contract in this scenario in 2016 is $3,466.67, derived as follows:

- Minimum monthly deductible = $2,600 statutory minimum family annual deductible divided by twelve months = $216.67
- Sixteen-month plan year minimum deductible = $216.67 monthly minimum deductible multiplied by sixteen months = <u>$3,466.67</u>

If your plan has a deductible less than this amount, you are not covered by an HSA-qualified plan during your first plan year (and therefore cannot contribute to an HSA). On your first renewal, though, your plan will be qualified because your new deductible year will be twelve months, and the statutory minimum annual deductible will not have to be adjusted.

As an example of the latter situation above, your plan could have a permanent deductible carryover feature. Under this provision, any deductible expenses that you incur during the final three months of the deductible year are applied to that year's deductible and also credited toward the following year's deductible. Insurers rarely apply this provision to HSA-qualified plans precisely because the health plan deductible must be 25% higher than the statutory minimum annual deductible, as follows:

- Minimum monthly deductible = the statutory minimum family annual deductible of $2,600 divided by twelve months = $216.67
- Fifteen-month plan year minimum deductible = the monthly minimum deductible of $216.67 multiplied by fifteen months = $3,250.00

These adjusted minimum deductibles do not impact the amount that you can contribute to your HSA. Prior to the 2007 tax year, you would have had to adjust your HSA contribution as well. Contributions were limited to the lower of the deductible or the statutory maximum annual deductible. A $3,000 family deductible on a plan with a three-month deductible carryover would result in a monthly contribution of $200 ($3,000 divided by a fifteen-month deductible). Since the IRS recognizes a contribution year of twelve months, the maximum contribution would have been $200 per month times twelve months or $2,400. The deductible carryover provision would have automatically reduced your maximum HSA contribution by 25%, even if you did not benefit from the deductible carryover. The HOPE Act, passed by Congress in December 2006 and effective January 1, 2007, eliminated this calculation by allowing you to contribute up to the statutory maximum annual contribution, regardless of your health plan deductible. *IRS Notice 2004-50, Q&A 24.*

Qualified plans sold on a fully insured basis must be approved by the insurance commissioner in the state in which they are sold. The plans must meet the mandates, rules, and regulations of those states in addition to the federal requirements. While Congress sets, and the IRS adjusts, the framework for an HSA-qualified plan design (minimum deductible, maximum out-of-pocket, range of services subject to the deductible, full coverage for certain preventive services), HSA-qualified plans sold on an insured basis must be approved by the insurance regulators in the state in which they are sold. The plans must include state mandates, guidelines and any other requirements that the state imposes.

When HSAs were introduced, mandates created issues in some states because some state mandates conflicted with the federal HSA framework. Example: All non-preventive treatments must be subject to the deductible under an HSA-qualified plan. If a state mandate required insurers to cover the full cost of treatment for lead-paint poisoning or sexually transmitted diseases for teenagers, these mandates would conflict with federal HSA requirements. In these cases, no insurer could offer an HSA-qualified plan in that state. Some states had to adjust certain mandates—either altering or eliminating them, or not applying them to HSA-qualified plans—so that their residents could enjoy the benefits of the HSA program.

KEY POINTS IN THIS CHAPTER

- An HSA-qualified plan must cover all non-preventive services subject to a deductible. Your policy cannot pay for any service that diagnoses or treats an injury, condition, or illness until you've paid for those services up to the value of the deductible. If your plan covers any services except certain preventive services in full or after a copay, the plan is not an HSA-qualified plan and you are not eligible to contribute to an HSA account.
- Prescription drugs must be subject to the deductible. Your insurer may have a list of preventive prescriptions covered outside the deductible (either covered in full or subject to different cost-sharing, such as copay or coinsurance).
- Certain preventive services must be covered in full as a result of provisions in the Affordable Care Act.
- HSA-qualified plans have a minimum deductible and an out-of-pocket maximum. The out-of-pocket maximum is the ceiling on what you must pay for covered services and applies to in-network services only. Your plan may have a lower out-of-pocket maximum, just as your deductible may be higher than the statutory minimum.
- The minimum deductible assumes a twelve-month deductible year. If your plan has a different deductible year—because of carryover credits or a one-time look-back when you enroll in the plan—the plan must meet an adjusted minimum deductible to remain an HSA-eligible plan.
- Your HSA-qualified plan may or may not offer coverage for out-of-network providers.

Consumer Checklist

✓ Verify that your plan is HSA-qualified. If the name of the plan does not include "HSA," check with your insurer or the final authority, your state's insurance commissioner.

✓ Check whether the deductible is *aggregate* (*umbrella*) or *embedded* if you have family coverage. The difference in your financial responsibility can be huge, particularly if the deductible is high and only one family member incurs high deductible expenses. A plan with a $10,000 deductible is more palatable for a family with one individual who is a high healthcare utilizer if the plan has an embedded individual deductible of $5,000.

✓ Check whether the in-network and out-of-network deductibles and out-of-pocket maximums are *combined* or *separate* if your plan covers out-of-network services. A separate out-of-network deductible is an additional disincentive to receive care from providers who are not contracted with your health plan. If the network is not comprehensive, or if you or a family member suffers from a rare condition for which specialists are not available in-network (or just do not contract with any insurers), your financial responsibility will increase dramatically if the in-network and out-of-network deductibles and out-of-pocket maximums are not combined.

✓ Review your level of coverage after you reach the deductible. Are services subject to other cost-sharing (a fixed copay, a percentage coinsurance) or covered in full? You want to know your true ceiling in a worst-case scenario year. Co-insurance (you pay, say, 20% of the remaining bill after the deductible) can add up quickly and bring you to the out-of-pocket maximum if you have an extended hospitalization or major course of treatment.

✓ Make sure you are not paying separate deductibles for medical and prescription drug and/or behavioral health services. If these services are not integrated under a single deductible, you'll be paying double or triple the statutory minimum annual deductible, which will drive your out-of-pocket costs higher.

✓ Review coverage for preventive services. Some must be covered in full under federal law, while insurers have latitude in how they cover other select preventive services. Your insurance contract will spell out exactly which services are covered in full. You do not want to be surprised after undergoing a routine physical to be hit with unexpected bills for lab tests that are subject to the deductible.

✓ Review whether preventive prescriptions are covered outside the deductible. This richer level of coverage can have a major impact on your out-of-pocket costs if you take prescriptions to prevent the onset of symptoms for a disease.

TEST YOUR KNOWLEDGE

1. **Your plan has a $5,000 family deductible, with each family member's deductible capped at $2,000. Is this an HSA-qualified plan?**

   A. Yes. The $5,000 deductible is higher than the statutory minimum of $2,600 in 2016.

   B. No. HSA-qualified plans cannot have an individual (embedded) deductible on a family contract.

   C. Yes. The individual deductible exceeds the $1,300 (2016 figure) self-only minimum deductible.

   D. No. The individual deductible must exceed the statutory minimum deductible on a family contract ($2,600 in 2016).

2. **Your self-only plan has an out-of-network level of benefits, with an out-of-pocket maximum of $10,000 out-of-network. Based on this fact alone, can this be an HSA-qualified plan?**

   A. Yes. The statutory maximum out-of-pocket applies to in-network services only.
   B. No. The out-of-pocket maximum cannot exceed $6,550.
   C. No. An HSA-qualified plan cannot provide benefits outside the network, except for urgent and emergent care.
   D. Yes, as long as any expenses above $6,550 are subject to coinsurance, so that the insurer begins to pay a portion of each claim.

3. **Your plan covers certain prescriptions outside the deductible. Is this an HSA-qualified plan?**

   A. No. All drugs must be subject to the deductible.
   B. Yes, if the drugs are preventive.
   C. Yes. Prescription drugs can be covered outside the deductible, as long as the prescription drug benefit is administered by a PBM.
   D. Yes, but only if you are required to pay something—copay or coinsurance—when you purchase the drug.

4. **Your plan has a $2,600 family deductible and a provision that applies credits for the last three months' deductible incurred the prior year. Is this an HSA-qualified plan?**

   A. Yes. The plan meets the statutory minimum annual deductible.
   B. No. HSA-qualified plans cannot have deductible credits.

    C. No. HSA-qualified plans can have deductible credits, but the statutory minimum annual deductible must be adjusted to reflect the additional months of deductible credit.

    D. Yes. An HSA-qualified plan can allow a deductible credit of no more than three months.

5. **Your plan charges no copay for a routine physical and a $25 copay for a routine eye exam. Based on this information alone, can this be an HSA-qualified plan?**

    A. Yes. A routine eye exam is preventive and can be covered outside the deductible.

    B. No. It violates the ACA, since all preventive services must be covered in full.

    C. No. It is not considered a preventive visit and therefore must be subject to the deductible.

    D. No. It must cover all preventive services subject to the same member cost-sharing.

TEST YOUR KNOWLEDGE ANSWERS

1. D. An HSA-qualified family contract cannot begin to pay benefits to any family member until the family has met at least the statutory minimum annual deductible ($2,600 in 2016).

2. A. The out-of-pocket maximum applies to in-network services only.

3. B. Insurers are allowed to cover select preventive services—including some prescription drugs—outside the deductible.

4. C. The deductible must be adjusted upward to reflect the longer deductible year of fifteen months. In this case, the minimum monthly deductible ($2,600 annual minimum divided by 12) is $216.67. Multiply that

figure by fifteen months (twelve months, plus three months' credit) to arrive at the minimum deductible of $3,250.

5. A. A routine eye exam is a preventive service. The ACA does not include this visit in its list of preventive services that must be covered in full. Therefore, an insurer can cover it as it wishes—subject to the deductible, subject to copay, subject to coinsurance or covered in full.

HEALTH SAVINGS ACCOUNTS

The balance of this book shifts from the health plan discussed in chapter 1 and focuses on the Health Savings Account. You are new entering the world of finance and investments, of IRS regulations and tax savings, of interest rates, dividends, and fees.

This chapter is short. It is just long enough to give you some basic information so that you'll understand HSAs in their proper context. We'll take a deeper dive into these topics in later chapters.

HSAs are offered by trustees or custodians. While there are legal differences in the fiduciary responsibilities of trustees and custodians, they perform the same duties in managing HSAs. This book refers to trustees and custodians collectively as "trustees."

An HSA is a tax-advantaged account designed to save and pay for certain health-related expenses tax-free. In practical terms, an HSA is a checking account with three distinct tax advantages: 1) on deposits (contributions), 2) on account balance growth and 3) qualified withdrawals (distributions). It may also include investment options for long-term saving. *IRS Notice 2004-2, Q&A 1.*

Contributions to an HSA are tax-free or tax-deductible. The money that you deposit into your HSA, up to certain annual limits, is not included in your taxable income for that year. This provision allows you to defer a portion of your compensation dollar that otherwise would be taxed and diverting the full $1 to your HSA. *IRC Section 223(a)* and *IRS Notice 2004-2, Q&A 17.*

Account balances do not expire and grow tax-deferred. Funds that you do not use in a particular year are available for your use in future years (some refer to this as "rolling over" into a new year). And as your account grows with interest and perhaps investment gains, you defer taxes on any earnings on the account growth at least until you withdraw the money. *IRC Section 223(e)(1).*

Withdrawals from your HSA are tax-free if used for an eligible expense. You can make tax-free withdrawals (the IRS refers to them as "distributions") for qualified medical, dental, and vision expenses, as well as over-the-counter supplies and equipment, over-the-counter drugs and medicine with a valid prescription, and certain insurance premiums. When you make distributions for eligible expenses, your account growth (on which taxes are deferred) is tax-free as well. *IRC Section 223(f) (1)* and *IRS Notice 2004-2, Q&A 25.*

You may withdraw money for purposes that are not IRS-eligible. In this case, your contributions remain tax-free in the year they were made, your account growth remains tax-deferred, but you must include your distribution as taxable income in the year withdrawn and pay a 20% penalty, if applicable. While HSAs are designed to reimburse eligible expenses, you have the ability to make withdrawals for any purpose at any time. Your HSA trustee cannot draft a trust agreement that restricts your right to make distributions for any expenses. If your distribution is not for an eligible expense, you must include the amount of the distribution as taxable income in that tax year. In addition, if you are under age sixty-five and not disabled, you pay a 20% penalty on your total distribution for non-eligible expenses. *IRC Section 223(f)(2)* and *IRS Notice 2004-2, Q&A 25.*

An HSA is a trust agreement. That simply means that the account itself is subject to certain state laws that govern trusts. This legal distinction does not change the fact that it is your money in the account and that you are responsible for managing the account in compliance with federal tax rules. *IRC Section 223(d)(1)* and *IRS Notice 2004-2, Q&A 1.*

You must work with an HSA trustee. You cannot merely designate a personal checking account as your HSA. An HSA is a trust, and you must work with a trustee who manages the account in accordance with IRS guidelines and regulations. You may choose your own trustee, even if your employer or health plan directs funds to a trustee of their choice. *IRC Section 223(d)(1)* and *IRS Notice 2004-2, Q&A 1.*

HSA trustees must be approved by the IRS. Trustees are usually banks, investment companies (such as brokerages and mutual fund companies), and insurance companies. Banks and credit unions are automatically approved as HSA trustees. Non-bank trustees must meet the same criteria as IRA trustees by demonstrating to the IRS that they are qualified fiduciaries, can account for transactions accurately and understand HSA rules. *IRS Notice 2004-2, Q&A 9.*

An HSA is an individual account. As with an IRA, a single person owns an HSA. There is no "Addams Family HSA" or "Brady Bunch HSA." HSAs are accounts owned by an individual who is solely responsible for the account. Note: Your HSA trustee may allow you to designate other people who can draw on your HSA balances and one person's HSA may be used for the family contribution limit in most cases. *IRC Section 223(d)(1)* and *IRS Notice 2004-50, Q&A 63.*

You can own more than one HSA. In fact, you can own as many as you wish. And when you are pursuing specific financial strategies, a second HSA might make sense. For most people, one HSA alone provides all the benefits that an HSA program offers without the burden and cost of managing multiple accounts. *IRS Notice 2004-50, Q&A 64.*

KEY POINTS IN THIS CHAPTER

- An HSA is legally a trust that you establish with a trustee, but in practical terms most people use it as they would an interest-bearing checking account. Chapter 8 provides you with more information.
- HSAs are triple-tax-advantaged accounts, with tax-free (or tax-deductible) contributions, tax-deferred growth and tax-free distributions for eligible expenses. You'll learn more in Chapter 4 (*Contributions*) and Chapter 5 (*Distributions*).
- You can make withdrawals for an expense that is not HSA-eligible, but you lose the benefit of tax-free distributions and in most cases incur a penalty as well. Chapter 5 provides more information.

CONSUMER CHECKLIST

- ✓ Be sure that you deal with only an IRS-approved trustee. You can reasonably assume that any institution advertising an HSA program is an IRS-approved trustee or is an administrative service working directly with an IRS-approved trustee. You'll learn more about trustees in chapter 8.
- ✓ Be sure that you understand which expenses are eligible for tax-free/penalty-free distributions. You'll learn more in chapter 5.

TEST YOUR KNOWLEDGE

1. **Which of the following statements about your HSA is *not* true?**

    A. Your HSA is a trust agreement.
    B. Your HSA account growth is subject to federal income taxes.

C. Your HSA contributions are excluded from your taxable income.

D. Your unused HSA balances roll over for future use.

2. **You want to own more than one HSA. Which of the following statements is true?**

A. You cannot legally own more than one HSA.

B. While you cannot own more than one HSA trust, you can designate a personal checking account as a second HSA.

C. The IRS sets no limit on the number of HSAs that you own.

D. You must apply to the IRS for an exception to open a second HSA, showing cause as to why you need two HSAs.

3. **Your local bank offers a free checking account. You want to open a free checking account and designate it as your HSA. Which of the following statements is true?**

A. You can do so as long as the bank is an IRS-approved HSA trustee.

B. You cannot do so. A checking account does not qualify as an HSA trust.

C. You cannot do so unless your employer has a written agreement with that bank to use checking accounts as HSAs for its employees.

D. You can do so, but the burden is on you to keep your account in compliance with HSA regulations.

4. **You and your wife are both HSA eligible and want to open a joint HSA. Which of the following statements is true?**

A. HSAs are individual accounts only.

B. You can have a joint HSA with a spouse only if the spouse is HSA-eligible.

C. If you want your spouse to have access to HSA balances to pay eligible expenses, the only way to do so is with a joint HSA.

D. Joint HSAs are not allowed unless the trustee has made special provisions with the IRS to offer this option.

Test Your Knowledge Answers

1. B. Balances grow tax-deferred and become tax-free when you make distributions for eligible expenses.

2. C. HSA-eligible individuals can own more than one HSA, but in most cases, there is no advantage to doing so.

3. B. An HSA is a special account governed by a specific trust agreement. A personal checking account does not qualify.

4. A. HSAs are individual accounts only.

HSA Eligibility

To be eligible to contribute to an HSA account (HSA-eligible), you must be covered by an HSA-qualified plan. This coverage represents the most basic (and generally best understood) eligibility criterion. If you are not covered by an HSA-qualified plan, you fail to meet the foundational eligibility criterion to establish or contribute to an HSA. *IRC Section 223(c)(1)* and *IRS Notice 2004-2, Q&A 2.*

If you are enrolled in more than one health plan, all health plans must be qualified plans in order for you to be HSA-eligible. You are allowed to be covered by more than one health plan and become or remain HSA-eligible. Most individuals believe that they are enrolled in only one health plan: the health insurance that they purchase through their employer or in the individual market. As you'll see as you continue reading, though, you may actually be covered by a second plan that you never thought of as a health plan. *IRC Section 223(c)(1)(A)(ii).*

You become HSA-eligible as of the first day of the first month that you meet all HSA eligibility criteria. The day that you meet HSA eligibility criteria is merely the first day that you become eligible to be eligible to establish and contribute to an HSA. Confused? The rule is simple. The IRS determines HSA eligibility based on your status as of the first day of a month. If you start a new job March 25 and enroll in an HSA-qualified plan immediately and meet all HSA eligibility criteria, you do not become HSA-eligible until the first day of the first month following that date, or April 1. You need to understand this rule because, as you'll see later, in this scenario, you cannot establish your HSA until April 1, and you are never able to reimburse any eligible expenses that you incur on the health plan before April 1 from your HSA on a tax-free basis. *IRC Section 223 (c)(1)(A) (i), IRS Notice 2004-2, Q&A 2* and *IRS Notice 2004-50, Q&A 11.*

If you lose HSA eligibility after the first day of the month, you remain HSA-eligible for the remainder of that month. You may lose your coverage under an HSA-qualified plan or lose your HSA eligibility for a variety of reasons that we'll explore in a moment. If you lose your eligibility after the first day of the month, you remain eligible for the remainder of that month, however. In this case, the "first day of the month" rule, which works against you in the previous situation above, works to your advantage here. You can change jobs September 2 and enroll immediately in your new employer's non-HSA-qualified health plan. Even though you cease to meet the HSA eligibility criteria as of September 2, you remain HSA-eligible through the end of September and can, as you'll learn in the contribution section, make a full HSA contribution for September. *IRC Section 223(c) (1)(A)(i)* and *IRS Notice 2004-2, Q&A 2.*

HSA eligibility is determined on an individual basis. You can be HSA-eligible even when other family members are not, whether you cover them on your HSA-qualified plan or not. When it comes to determining your HSA eligibility, the IRS looks at you and you alone. Regardless of other family members' situations (disqualifying coverage is discussed below), your coverage alone determines whether you are HSA-eligible. Even if members of your family are enrolled in disqualifying coverage (such as Medicare, discussed below), you are not impacted by the factor that makes them ineligible, as long as you are not entitled to reimbursement through that coverage too. *IRS Notice 2008-59, Q&A 11.*

An individual does not have to be the health plan subscriber to be HSA-eligible. A health plan subscriber is the individual who purchases the policy, either through his or her employer or directly from the insurance company or a third party. If you are purchasing the plan through your employer, for example, you are the subscriber, and other individuals covered under the policy are health plan "members." In some cases, the HSA-qualified health plan subscriber does not meet the HSA eligibility criteria (discussed below). In these situations, another member covered under the plan may be able to meet the eligibility criteria and establish an HSA that will reimburse all family members' eligible expenses tax-free. *IRC Section 223(c)(1)(A).*

Permitted Coverage and Other Allowable Situations

You can be enrolled in a dental plan and remain HSA-eligible. Since dental insurance does not constitute major medical coverage, enrolling in a dental plan does not impact your HSA eligibility. *IRC Section 223(c)(1)(B)(ii)* and *IRS Notice 2004-2, Q&A 6.*

You can enroll in a vision plan and remain HSA-eligible. As with dental insurance above, a vision program does not provide major medical benefits. Thus, coverage under a vision plan does not disqualify you from becoming or remaining HSA-eligible. *IRC Section 223(c)(1)(B)(ii)* and *IRS Notice 2004-2, Q&A 6.*

You can enroll in hospitalization and specific-illness and accident plans and remain HSA-eligible. These policies, offered by some employers as "voluntary benefits" (which usually means that you pay the entire premium and the sponsoring company requires a certain percentage of the work force to enroll before finalizing the plans), do not provide medical reimbursement. Instead, they pay you a certain flat sum or daily amount when you are hospitalized, are diagnosed with an illness covered by the policy (cancer is the most common covered illness) or are involved in an accident. You then can use these funds to pay medical expenses subject to the deductible, reimburse other costs associated with care, or use the money to pay personal expenses. Because the payments are not tied to the cost of specific treatment, they are not considered medical reimbursement, even if you use the money to pay providers for services related to that hospitalization, illness, or accident and subject to cost-sharing under your medical plan.

These voluntary plans may become more attractive as your out-of-pocket expenses increase under an HSA-qualified plan. Beware, though, that you can incur high costs for outpatient treatment for an illness or condition that does not result from an accident and is not covered by a specific-illness policy. In that case, you would pay premiums for your voluntary benefit, incur high expenses, and receive no voluntary policy payout. On the other hand, if you are covered by one or more of these policies, you may find your financial burden eased by a payment that covers a portion of what you owe your providers. *IRC Section 223(c)(3)(B and C), IRS Notice 2004-2, Q&A 6* and *IRS Notice 2004-50, Q&A 7.*

You do not lose your HSA eligibility if another party is responsible for covering some or all of your expenses due to the other party's liability. You are not penalized if you incur deductible expenses that are reimbursed by someone else because that person was at fault. Typical situations include worker's compensation (you are injured at work), homeowner's insurance (the neighbors' dog bites you or you slip on your neighbor's steps) and auto insurance (another driver is a fault when you are injured in an accident). In addition to these instances in which someone else's insurance policy reimburses your expenses, you do not lose your HSA eligibility if you sue someone for causing your injuries and win a judgment. *IRC Section 223(c)(3)(A)* and *IRS Notice 2004-2, Q&A 6.*

You do not lose your HSA eligibility if you are enrolled in a discount card program that allows you to receive discounted

rates from a provider. This situation occurs most commonly with a drug discount card. An individual may purchase (or an employer may purchase for employees) a card that allows the individual to receive a discount when he purchases a prescription drug. In other cases, presentation of a group membership card (union, credit union, fraternal organization, or senior citizen organization membership card) may result in your receiving a discount negotiated by the card issuer. The discount is absorbed by the entity dispensing the good or service, and because it is a discount, it does not constitute a reimbursement. *IRS Notice 2004-50, Q&A 9.*

You do not lose your HSA eligibility if you receive and pay for services outside your health plan, as long as you do not receive reimbursement from any source that's not permitted insurance or permitted coverage. A typical example is that you take advantage of a chain pharmacy's discount program, which provides prescriptions outside of insurance at a flat fee of perhaps $3 to $4 for a thirty-day supply or $10 for a ninety-day supply. You can take advantage of these programs without losing your HSA eligibility (and in some cases, your insurer may accept a claim from you and apply the amount to your deductible). Another example is if you pay cash for a service not covered by your health plan (acupuncture, biofeedback) or a benefit (chiropractic care, outpatient therapy) with a limit that you have exhausted under the insurance plan. Insurance generally will not cover these expenses (except perhaps if you appeal), but you can pay for them with personal funds and not compromise your HSA eligibility. *IRS Notice 2004-50, Q&A 9.*

MEDICARE AND MEDICAID

If you are enrolled in any part of Medicare, you are no longer HSA-eligible, since Medicare plan designs do not meet the criteria for a qualified plan. If you are not yet enrolled in Medicare and want to become or remain HSA-eligible, you must delay enrollment in Medicare when you are initially eligible to become or remain HSA-eligible. If you are already enrolled in any Part of Medicare (individuals often enroll in Part A when they turn age sixty-five, though enrollment is not automatic if you are not receiving Social Security benefits), you are not HSA-eligible.

In this situation, it is important to remember that an individual does not have to be the health plan subscriber to be HSA-eligible. If you enroll in Part A and continue to work while you cover yourself and your spouse on your employer's HSA-qualified plan, your spouse may be HSA-eligible. In that case, he or she can open an HSA, either or both of you can contribute to his or her HSA and he or she can reimburse eligible expenses that either of you incur. *IRC Section 223((b)(7)* and *IRS Notice 2004-50, Q&A 2.*

You do not lose your HSA eligibility if a family member is enrolled in Medicare. All Medicare policies are individual contracts. A family member's enrollment in Medicare (which issues individual policies only) does not impact your HSA eligibility, as long as you yourself are not enrolled in Medicare. *IRS Notice 2008-59, Q&A 11.*

If you are enrolled in Medicaid or another publicly funded insurance program, you are not HSA-eligible. These public programs generally do not meet the design criteria of an HSA-qualified plan, although some states are beginning to offer or are considering offering HSA programs for Medicaid participants. An individual enrolled in both an HSA-qualified plan and Medicaid or another similar state or federal government program is enrolled in two health plans, at least one of which is not a qualified plan. Remember, though, that as long as *you* are not enrolled in one of these programs (which cover subscribers only— they are not family plans) and meet other eligibility criteria, you can establish and contribute to your own HSA.

If you are enrolled in one of these programs but another family member (such as your spouse) meets all HSA eligibility criteria, your spouse can establish and contribute to an HSA (and may be able to reimburse your expenses—see the *Distribution* chapter for more information). *IRS Notice 2004-50, Q&A 4* and *IRS Notice 2008-59, Q&A 6 and Q&A 11*.

You do not lose eligibility because a family member is enrolled in Medicaid or similar government coverage. Medicaid, S-CHIP (State Children's Health Insurance Program, a federal-state jointly funded program that covers children) and other similar programs enroll individuals only. Members of your family can be enrolled in these products without compromising your HSA eligibility. *IRS Notice 2008-59, Q&A 11*

VA, TRICARE and Other Government Programs

If you receive non-preventative, non-service-connected care from a Department of Veterans Services (VA) facility, you can lose your HSA eligibility for a period of three months. On July 31, 2015, President Obama signed HR 3236, the "Surface Transportation and Veterans Health Care Choice Improvement Act of 2015" into law. That law removes the provision in the Internal Revenue Code that disqualified people receiving non-preventive benefits for service-connected disabilities from the Veterans Administration from contributing to Health Savings Accounts starting January 1, 2016. (The VA will define the exact definition of "service-connected care" and how veterans can distinguish care categories before implementation, but that information is not available at the time of this writing.) If you are otherwise HSA-eligible, you can regain your HSA eligibility as of the first day of the first month after the three-month period immediately following the end of your cycle of care through the VA. Thus, being eligible to receive care through the VA system (which offers care with cost-sharing that does not meet the standards for an HSA-qualified plan) does not in itself disqualify you from being HSA-eligible. Rather, accessing care (a situation that you can control) for non-preventive services compromises your eligibility temporarily. There may be times when you benefit financially by receiving treatment through the VA rather than have those services subject to the deductible through your HSA-qualified plan, even if you lose HSA eligibility temporarily. IRS Notice 2004-50, Q&A, HR 3236, the "Surface Transportation and Veterans Health Care Choice Improvement Act of 2015"

If you receive services that are considered select preventive care, you can receive those services through any provider (including a VA facility) and remain HSA-eligible. If a VA facility is more convenient for select preventive care, you can receive care in the VA system and not lose your HSA eligibility. Both the VA and your HSA-qualified plan cover many select preventive services in full as a result of provisions of the ACA, but there may be some situations in which your HSA-qualified plan or the VA covers a preventive service in full but the other requires a level of cost-sharing. *IRS Notice 2008-59, Q&A 9.*

If you receive non-preventive care through an Indian Health Service (IHS) facility, you lose your HSA eligibility for a period of three months following that care. The rules are the same as for the VA system (above) except that the new law provided no relief for users of the Indian Health Service. *IRS Notice 2012-14.*

HSA-eligible individuals who receive services that are considered preventive care can receive those services through any provider (including an IHS facility) and remain HSA-eligible. Again, see the parallel passage about the VA (above), as the rules are identical. *IRS Notice 2012-14.*

If you are enrolled in TRICARE, the federal government insurance program for active and retired military personnel, you are not HSA-eligible. TRICARE plans do not meet the requirements of an HSA-qualified plan. Regardless of whether or not you are also enrolled in an HSA-qualified plan, your enrollment in TRICARE, which does not have an HSA-qualified option, makes you ineligible to establish and contribute to an HSA. *IRS Notice 2004-50, Q&A 6.*

Health Flexible Spending Arrangements (Health FSAs)

A Health FSA is an employer-sponsored program through which employees can elect to receive a portion of their compensation in nontaxable benefits rather than cash. Employees make an annual election, and the employer withholds this amount from their paychecks in equal installments throughout the year. The withholding occurs before the money is taxed. For the typical employee subject to 30% combined federal and state tax withholding, every dollar that he elects to place in a Health FSA reduces his take-home pay by about 70 cents, but the full dollar goes into the Health FSA and is available to the employee to spend on eligible expenses.

Expenses eligible for reimbursement through a general Health FSA include medical, prescription drug, dental and vision expenses, as well as over-the-counter equipment and supplies (and over-the-counter drugs and medicine with a valid prescription) and certain health-related travel and parking expenses.

A Limited-Purpose Health FSA reimburses dental and vision expenses only, plus select preventive services that are not covered in full. A Post-Deductible Health FSA does not begin to pay benefits until the subscriber has met a deductible responsibility at least equal to the statutory minimum annual deductible for his contract type on an HSA-qualified plan.

If you are covered by a general Health FSA, you are not HSA-eligible. The IRS defines a Health FSA as a health plan. In the eyes of the IRS, your election of $2,000 to a Health FSA really is a $2,000 premium payment that you make to receive a $2,000 benefit. In this case, even if you are covered under an HSA-qualified plan as well, your general Health FSA does not meet the design requirements of an HSA-qualified plan. You thus have disqualifying coverage and are not HSA-eligible, nor is your spouse (see next paragraph). *IRS Rev. Rul. 2004-45, Situation 1.*

If your spouse is enrolled in a general Health FSA through his or her employer, neither you nor your spouse is HSA-eligible. A general Health FSA reimburses medical, prescription drug, dental, vision, and certain over-the-counter item expenses of the plan subscriber, spouse, and dependent children. It does not matter whether you or your spouse is the general Health FSA subscriber. Under the federal tax code, you and your spouse are automatically covered under your own or your spouse's general Health FSA by virtue of your relationship as husband and wife.

If you are offered an opportunity to enroll in an HSA-qualified plan during your own (or your spouse's) general Health FSA plan year, you cannot opt out of the Health FSA to become HSA-eligible immediately. You are allowed to enroll in, disenroll from, or change your election to a Health FSA midyear only with a qualifying life-change event (such as marriage, divorce, birth, adoption, or death). Your change must be consistent with the event (so that, for example, if you marry, you typically cannot add one or more people to your health plan and then *decrease* your Health FSA election). Merely being offered the opportunity to enroll in a general Health FSA is not a qualifying event, and you cannot disenroll from your own (nor can your spouse disenroll from his or her) general Health FSA midyear so that you can gain HSA eligibility upon enrollment in the HSA-qualified plan.

If you have a health plan anniversary and general Health FSA with a different plan year, you have as many as three options:

- Choose not to enroll in an HSA-qualified plan.
- Enroll in the HSA-qualified plan, understand that you will not be HSA-eligible until the end of the general Health FSA plan year, and pay any HSA-eligible expenses from the remaining funds in your Health FSA (you'll get the same tax benefit, though you may run out of Health FSA funds because you made your election

based on not having an HSA-qualified health plan as your insurance coverage).

- Delay enrollment in the HSA-qualified plan for a year (if you have a choice of plans during open enrollment), choose not to participate in the general Health FSA the following year, understand that you'll have a period of time after the end of the general Health FSA plan year during which you cannot pay for eligible expenses with tax-free dollars, and then enroll in the HSA-qualified plan on your next health plan anniversary date.

Your choice of strategies will depend on your health plan options and the amount of overlap between the general Health FSA and HSA plan years. For example, if your health plan anniversary is April 1 and your general Health FSA runs through December, the third option may make more sense. If your health plan anniversary is April 1 and the general Health FSA year runs through May 31, the second approach (with only a two-month gap during which you cannot reimburse eligible expenses tax-free) may be a better option.

If you are or your spouse is enrolled in a general Health FSA at the time of enrollment in an HSA-qualified plan, you cannot establish or begin to make contributions to or receive tax-free reimbursements from an HSA until the end of the general Health FSA plan year.

If your general Health FSA has a grace period, you must act prior to the end of the twelve-month plan year to become HSA-eligible before the beginning of the grace period. Employers are permitted to add a grace period to their Health FSAs. A grace period is an additional 2½ months after the close of the twelve-month plan year during which participants continue to accumulate expenses eligible for reimbursement out of that year's Health FSA election, thus reducing participant forfeitures. This is a nice benefit to employees, who have 14½ months to accumulate expenses that they can reimburse with that year's elections. If your Health FSA has a grace period, you must act decisively to become HSA-eligible at the end of the twelve-month year. You must spend your entire Health FSA election so that your FSA administrator's books show you with zero cash balance prior to the end of the twelve-month year (prior to the beginning of the grace period). If you spend your entire election before the end of the twelve-month year, you become HSA-eligible immediately at the end of the twelve-month Health FSA year (assuming that you are otherwise HSA-eligible).

If you carry any balance (even a penny) into the grace period, you cannot become HSA-eligible until the end of the grace period. If you reduce your balance to zero by the middle of the first month of the grace period, for example, you cannot become HSA-eligible as of the first day of the second month of the grace period. A grace period typically runs 2½ months, carrying it through the middle of a month. Since HSA eligibility is determined as of the first day of a month, you cannot become HSA-eligible until the first day of the following month (three full months after the end of the twelve-month Health FSA plan year).

If you are not HSA-eligible, you can use your Health FSA funds to reimburse any expenses incurred during the grace period. *IRC Section 223(c)(1)(B)(iii) as amended* and *Health Opportunity Patient Empowerment Act of 2006, Section 5(b)*.

If your Health FSA includes a rollover of up to $500, you need to act to protect your HSA eligibility. In October 2013, the IRS ruled that employers could amend their Health FSA plans to allow a rollover of up to $500 into the following plan year. Under this provision, participants can roll over a limited balance amount for an unlimited time period. (By contrast, the grace period allows an unlimited balance amount rollover for a limited time.)

The IRS says there are three ways to act to preserve your HSA eligibility when transitioning from a Health FSA with a rollover feature.

First, as with the grace period, if the Health FSA participant spends her entire FSA balance by the end of the Health FSA plan year, she can become HSA-eligible as soon as she enrolls in the HSA-qualified plan (assuming that she is otherwise HSA-eligible).

Second, employers may allow employees choose before the end of the plan year to transfer funds into a Limited-Purpose FSA. Employers are also allowed to automatically move employees' unused dollars into a Limited-Purpose FSA for all who select an HSA-qualified plan in the following plan year.

Finally, the IRS allows for employers to give the option for an employee to simply decline or waive participation in the balance rollover provision to maintain HSA eligibility. (IRS Memorandum 201413005 dated 3/28/14).

You can enroll in a Limited-Purpose Health FSA and not lose your HSA eligibility. Your employer can offer a Limited-Purpose Health FSA, which reimburses dental and vision expenses only. Since these expenses are "permitted coverage" under Section 223, an individual can have this coverage and remain HSA-eligible. The Limited-Purpose Health FSA is created and administered by the FSA administrator; an individual subscriber cannot turn his employer's general Health FSA into a Limited-Purpose Health FSA merely by not submitting medical, prescription drug and other ineligible claims for reimbursement. *IRS Rev. Rul. 2004-45, Situation 2.*

You can enroll in a Post-Deductible Health FSA and remain HSA-eligible. A Post-Deductible Health FSA reimburses all FSA-eligible expenses once your deductible expenses under your HSA-qualified plan exceed the statutory minimum annual deductible ($1,300 for a self-only and $2,600 for a family contract in 2016). If you are enrolled in a Post-Deductible Health FSA, you are enrolled in two health plans (a traditional health insurance plan and the Post-Deductible Health FSA), both of which are qualified plans. *IRS Rev. Rul. 2004-45, Situation 4.*

You do not lose HSA eligibility because you enroll in a dependent care Flexible Spending Arrangement. There are two distinct FSAs. One is the Health FSA, discussed above. The second is a Dependent Care Reimbursement Account (DCRA), which reimburses child care expenses (nursery, pre-school, after-school and summer day camp expenses for children under age thirteen) and certain expenses for watching children to age thirteen and older and certain older disabled dependents (including adults) while you (and your spouse, if you are married) work or go to school. Since the DCRA does not reimburse medical expenses, your participation in a DCRA program does not impact your HSA eligibility.

HEALTH REIMBURSEMENT ARRANGEMENTS (HRAS)

An HRA is an employer-funded program that allows employers to give employees tax-free reimbursements for certain eligible health-related expenses. The employer designs the program within IRS guidelines by setting the value of the HRA, the specific expenses to be reimbursed, whether to allow a rollover of unused funds and how to design the required continuation of coverage under the federal Consolidated Omnibus Budget Reconciliation Act of 1985 (COBRA).

A typical HRA, and the design that we'll use in the context of this discussion, is a program that reimburses a portion of the deductible expenses associated with a high deductible health plan. The IRS classifies an HRA as a group health plan, which has important implications for HSA eligibility. Employees covered by a high deductible health plan and an HRA have, in effect, coverage through two health plans.

If you can access reimbursements through your own or a spouse's general HRA, you are not HSA-eligible. Because an HRA is a health plan, it too must meet the design criteria for an HSA-qualified plan. A general HRA that reimburses, say, the first half of the health plan deductible, violates the minimum deductible rules of an HSA-qualified plan. *IRS Rev. Rul. 2004-45, Situation 1.*

You can be HSA-eligible if your employer offers a Post-Deductible HRA that does not begin to reimburse expenses until you've met the statutory minimum annual deductible for an HSA-qualified plan. A Post-Deductible HRA does not begin to pay any benefits until you've incurred at least $1,300 (self-only contract) or $2,600 (family contract) in deductible expenses (2016 figures). Under this scenario, you are covered by two health plans (an HSA-qualified insurance plan and a Post-Deductible HRA), both of which are HSA-qualified plans. You are responsible for the first portion of your deductible expenses before either the health plan or the HRA begins to reimburse your expenses. You can use HSA funds to reimburse these initial expenses before the health plan or the HRA begins to pay. *IRS Rev. Rul. 2004-45, Situation 4.*

Your employer can offer you certain other limited HRA programs that will not impact your HSA eligibility. These designs include a Limited-Purpose HRA (reimburses dental, vision, and preventive services only), a suspended HRA (you cannot access any accumulated funds now), or a retirement HRA (your accumulated unused balances are available only upon retirement). The Limited-Purpose HRA does not impact your HSA eligibility because reimbursement for dental, vision, and preventive services does not disqualify you, per the original HSA legislation. The suspended and retirement HRAs do not impact your HSA eligibility because you cannot access any balances in those accounts until sometime in the future. *IRS Rev. Rul. 2004-45, Situations 2 and 4.*

Your limited HRA must be designed as a limited HRA. You can retain HSA eligibility only if you are enrolled in a Post-Deductible, Limited-Purpose, suspended, or retirement HRA with a plan document setting the rules for reimbursement. You cannot be enrolled in a general HRA and promise to reimburse dental and vision expenses only, or promise not to seek reimbursement until you've met the statutory minimum annual deductible, or promise not to use this year's employer HRA allocation but instead roll it over to sometime in the future. The plan document must include plan rules that make the HRA a qualified limited HRA, and the HRA administrator must adhere to these rules in administering the HRA. *IRS Rev. Rul. 2004-45, Situation 2.*

KEY POINTS IN THIS CHAPTER

- Whether you are HSA-eligible for a month is determined by whether you are eligible on the first day of the month.
- Review your health coverage carefully. If you are married, review your spouse's coverage and benefits as well. Either of you could have coverage that would make both of you ineligible to participate in an HSA program, even if you are covered by an HSA-qualified plan.
- Your HSA eligibility is determined by coverage that reimburses *your* expenses. Other members of your family can be ineligible to participate in an HSA program (a spouse who's enrolled in Medicare, children who are tax dependents), but if the situation that makes them ineligible does not impact you, you can become or remain HSA-eligible.
- Individuals do not have to be health plan subscribers to be HSA-eligible. Anyone covered by an HSA-qualified

plan who meets all HSA eligibility criteria can open and contribute to an HSA but is not required to do so.

- Be very careful of participation in a Health FSA or HRA program offered by your or your spouse's employer. These programs, if not designed as limited reimbursement programs, can make you ineligible to open and contribute to an HSA, even if you are otherwise eligible.

- Also, remember that if your or your spouse's employer offers a Health FSA with a grace or rollover period, you need to spend that balance to zero before the end of the twelve-month plan year to become HSA-eligible at the beginning of the extended period.

- You can have certain other coverage and remain HSA-eligible. This permitted coverage and permitted insurance is a very specific and finite list.

CONSUMER CHECKLIST

✓ Make sure that your plan is an HSA-qualified plan. To know for certain, contact your state insurance commissioner.

✓ Do not enroll in Medicare when you are first eligible if you want to remain HSA-eligible. Once you enroll in any Part of Medicare, you are effectively locked out of further contributions to HSA program. Understand and weigh your options carefully before enrolling in Medicare (or before receiving Social Security benefits at age sixty-five or older, which automatically enrolls you in Medicare Part A).

✓ If you are entitled to receive care through the VA health care system, weigh the medical and financial benefits of receiving this non-preventive, non-service-connected care at a VA facility against the temporary loss of HSA eligibility.

✓ Review your benefit options carefully during your employer's open enrollment period to make sure that you do not enroll in a benefit that compromises your HSA eligibility. The most common situation is enrollment in your employer's general Health FSA program. Your employer should catch this mistake and make sure that you do not enroll, but you should not count on someone else to prevent this situation.

✓ Check with your spouse to make sure that he or she has not signed up for coverage that can disqualify you from HSA eligibility. The most common situation is that your spouse enrolls in a general Health FSA program that automatically entitles you, as the spouse, to reimbursement.

✓ If you are enrolling in an HSA-qualified plan and are enrolled in your (or your spouse's) employer's general Health FSA with a grace or rollover period, be sure you spend your entire election and post a zero balance as of the last day of the twelve-month plan year (before the extended period begins). Otherwise, you will not be able to be HSA-eligible until the first day of the third month after the end of the 2½-month grace period or in the case of a rollover, until the end of the plan year when the funds are exhausted.

Test Your Knowledge

1. **You are HSA-eligible. Your husband tells you that he's enrolled in his employer's general Health FSA plan. Which statement is true?**

    A. He's no longer HSA-eligible, but you remain HSA-eligible because you are not the Health FSA subscriber.

B. His Health FSA disqualifies both you and your husband from being HSA-eligible.

C. A Health FSA is permitted coverage, so his enrolling does not impact *your* HSA eligibility.

D. You remain HSA-eligible as long as you do not reimburse the same expense from both your Health FSA and HSA ("double dipping").

2. **After returning from a tour of duty in Afghanistan, you receive a mammogram at no cost to you at a VA clinic. Which statement is true?**

A. You lose your HSA eligibility for the balance of the calendar year.

B. You lose your HSA eligibility for three months.

C. You do not lose your HSA eligibility because a mammogram is a preventive service, and you can receive it through any provider.

D. You do not lose your HSA eligibility; Section 223(b)(ii) specifically allows *combat* veterans to remain HSA-eligible if they receive care through their local VA facility.

3. **You turn sixty-five and decide to remain working and covered by your employer's HSA-qualified plan, rather than retiring and enrolling in Social Security. Which statement is true?**

A. You are automatically enrolled in Part A at age sixty-five and therefore are no longer HSA-eligible.

B. You are automatically enrolled in Parts A and B at age sixty-five, and the HSA eligibility rules allow you to have this coverage and remain HSA-eligible.

C. You are not required to enroll in any Part of Medicare at age sixty-five. If you do not enroll, you remain HSA-eligible.

D. You are HSA-eligible as long as you have other coverage and receive no benefits from Medicare until you've met the minimum deductible for an HSA-qualified plan.

4. **You and your spouse are enrolled in your HSA-qualified plan. Your spouse is enrolled in Medicare. Which of the following statements is true?**

A. You both lose your HSA eligibility because of your spouse's enrollment in Medicare.

B. You are both HSA-eligible.

C. You remain HSA-eligible, but your spouse does not.

D. Your spouse is HSA-eligible, but you are not.

5. **You make an election into your employer's Limited-Purpose Health FSA. Which of the following expenses can you reimburse tax-free from your Limited-Purpose Health FSA?**

A. A prescription for an antibiotic.

B. A carpal tunnel syndrome splint.

C. A dental implant.

D. Teeth whitening.

6. **You are enrolled in an HSA-qualified plan and contribute to an HSA. Your wife's employer offers a dental HRA rather than a dental plan, and she enrolls. Which statement is true?**

A. You are not HSA-eligible because of your wife's HRA.

B. You are HSA-eligible because dental insurance or coverage is permitted under Section 223.

C. You are not HSA-eligible because an administrator cannot limit HRA reimbursement to dental services, and you could reimburse other expenses that would compromise your HSA eligibility.

D. You are HSA-eligible because it is your spouse's HRA, not yours.

7. **Your employer offers an HSA-qualified plan on its July 1 anniversary date. You want to enroll, but your wife has a general Health FSA that runs through December 31. What are the implications for you?**

A. You can enroll in the HSA-qualified plan. You are not HSA-eligible until the end of your wife's Health FSA plan year, but you can reimburse eligible expenses from her Health FSA.

B. You cannot enroll in the HSA-qualified plan because you are not HSA-eligible.

C. You can enroll in the HSA-qualified plan, but you cannot reimburse your deductible expenses tax-free from any account.

D. You can enroll in the HSA-qualified plan, but you cannot access care until the end of your wife's Health FSA plan year.

8. **Your husband turns sixty-five and remains the subscriber on his employer's HSA-qualified plan on which he covers you. He starts collecting Social Security benefits to supplement your income. Which statement is true?**

A. He remains HSA-eligible as long as he does not enroll in Medicare.

B. Both he and you are no longer HSA-eligible because he's automatically enrolled in Medicare Part A.

C. He's no longer HSA-eligible because his enrollment in Social Security triggers automatic enrollment in Medicare Part A, but you may be HSA-eligible, in which case you can open an HSA and make contributions.

D. He's no longer HSA-eligible because his enrollment in Social Security triggers his automatic enrollment in Medicare, and you cannot be HSA-eligible because you are not the subscriber.

9. **You purchase an HSA-qualified plan without prescription drug coverage. You purchase a drug discount card that provides you with a 20% discount on all purchases at leading chain pharmacies. What's the implication of your drug discount card?**

A. You can purchase prescriptions and remain HSA-eligible, since a discount card does not constitute coverage that conflicts with HSA-qualified plan guidelines.

B. You can purchase prescription drugs with the discount card only after you've met your statutory minimum annual deductible.

C. Individuals covered under an HSA-qualified plan are not eligible to purchase a drug discount card.

D. You can use the drug discount card only to purchase preventive prescriptions.

10. **You enroll your entire family on your HSA-qualified plan. Your wife starts a new job and is required to enroll in her employer's non-HSA-qualified plan, so she purchases an individual policy. What is the implication for your family?**

A. Her policy disqualifies both of you from being HSA-eligible.

B. Her individual policy does not impact anyone's HSA eligibility, since her primary coverage is through your HSA-qualified plan.

C. Her policy disqualifies her, but not you, from being HSA-eligible to make a family level contribution.

D. Her policy disqualifies you and her only if it begins to pay benefits to her before you reach the statutory minimum annual deductible on your HSA-qualified plan.

TEST YOUR KNOWLEDGE ANSWERS

1. B. A Health FSA automatically covers the subscriber (your husband), the subscriber's spouse (you) and any dependent children. Since both you and he are covered by this disqualifying coverage, neither of you is HSA-eligible.

2. C. You can access permitted preventive care without cost-sharing at any location without impacting your HSA eligibility.

3. C. You are not automatically enrolled in Medicare at age sixty-five. As long as you are not enrolled in any Part of Medicare, you remain HSA-eligible.

4. C. Medicare is an individual plan. Your spouse is not HSA-eligible, but since you cannot access benefits through your spouse's individual policy, you do not lose your HSA eligibility.

5. C. A Limited-Purpose Health FSA reimburses dental, vision, and preventive care only. Note: Teeth whitening is cosmetic, not medical, and therefore not eligible for tax-free reimbursement through any tax-advantaged account.

6. B. Dental coverage, whether through traditional dental insurance or a limited HRA, is permitted insurance.

7. A. You can enroll in an HSA-qualified plan whether you are HSA-eligible or not. And enrolling in an HSA-qualified plan does not limit your reimbursement options

to an HSA. If you have access to a Health FSA, you can reimburse eligible expenses tax-free from that account.

8. C. You automatically are enrolled in Medicare Part A when you receive Social Security benefits and are age sixty-five or older. Since Medicare offers individual coverage only, you cannot access benefits through Medicare and therefore are HSA-eligible if you meet all other eligibility criteria.

9. A. Discount cards are not insurance. Instead, the seller agrees to sell the item at a lower price to you, just as an insurer might negotiate with the same seller to offer discounts to insured members. You remain HSA-eligible.

10. C. Her individual policy provides coverage for her only. If you are otherwise HSA-eligible, you remain so, and because other members of the family are covered by your HSA plan, you can contribute to the family limit.

HSA Contributions (Deposits)

(All information contained in this section assumes an HSA-eligible individual.)

Contribution Limits

HSA contributions are either pre-tax or tax-deductible, depending on how you contribute. If your employer makes a contribution to your HSA, the employer receives the tax deduction, and your income is reduced by the contribution amount, giving you the same net tax benefit, with one exception we will discuss later. You receive deductions for contributions made by anyone else. *IRS Notice 2004-2, Q&A 16 and Q&A 17.*

Anyone can contribute to your HSA. While most contributions come from either your employer or you, anyone (your grandmother, a customer, a neighbor) can contribute to your HSA. A handful of states offer, or are evaluating, programs that make state taxpayer contributions to state employees' or Medicaid recipients' accounts when those individuals, who are eligible for state insurance programs, join an HSA program. *IRS Notice 2004-2, Q&A 11 and IRS Notice 2004-50, Q&A 28.*

The IRS sets annual limits on HSA contributions. HSA-eligible individuals are permitted to accept contributions from any source into their HSAs. The data period for calculating the inflation adjustments runs through March (reported by the Bureau of Labor Services in April of each year. The US Treasury Department is required to publish the inflation-adjusted amounts for the upcoming year for HSAs by June 1 each year.

With the exception of contributions from your employer (in which case the employer enjoys a tax deduction and that portion of your income is excluded), contributions you receive the tax deduction for any contributions to your HSA. *IRC Section 223(a), Tax Relief and Health Care Act of 2006 (P.L. 109-432).*

The contribution limits change annually. The limits are indexed annually to adjust for overall (not medical) inflation. The 2015 and 2016 statutory maximum annual contributions are as follows:

	2015	2016
• Self-only contract:	$3,350	$3,350
• Family contract:	$6,650	$6,750

HSA contribution limits are not tied to the health plan deductible. When HSAs were introduced, individuals could not contribute any more than the lesser of the health plan deductible or the statutory maximum annual contribution for a contract type. The Health Opportunity and Patient Education Act of 2006 changed the rules so that you can contribute up to the statutory maximum annual contribution irrespective of your health plan deductible. *HOPE Act, Section 3.*

Once you reach age fifty-five, you can make an additional annual $1,000 catch-up contribution to your HSAs. As with qualified retirement plans, you are allowed to increase your contributions as you grow older (though the catch-up contribution for qualified retirement plans kicks in five years earlier—at age fifty—and often is quite a bit greater than the $1,000 additional HSA contribution). This $1,000 figure, which is not adjusted for inflation, allows you to reduce your taxable income further and increase your HSA balance as you approach retirement. *IRC Section 223(b)(3)* and *IRS Notice 2004-2, Q&A 14.*

HSA contribution limits for nearly all taxpayers are based on a calendar year. While your health plan may have an anniversary date other than January 1, your HSA contributions are based on the calendar year. It may seem disjointed to have your health plan and HSA on different twelve-month periods, but remember that an HSA is a financial vehicle. As with other financial vehicles, the IRS measures tax consequences on the calendar (tax) year, regardless of when you purchased or increased your contribution to the financial vehicle. *IRS Rev. Proc. 2012-26, Section 3.*

You can make your annual contribution up to the due date of your personal income tax return for that year. You have 15½ months to make your contribution to your HSA for a given tax year, just as you do with an IRA. This flexibility helps you to maximize your contribution. When you make a contribution for the prior year, be sure to tell your trustee to apply the contribution to the previous year. Otherwise, a trustee will apply a contribution to the year that it is received. Your trustee typically provides some form of deposit slip or online selection for personal contributions that allows you to state the year to which to apply the contributions. Note: You usually cannot make contributions that apply to the prior year through pre-tax payroll contributions if your employer offers a Cafeteria Plan. *IRS Notice 2004-2, Q&A 21.*

If you lose your HSA eligibility during the calendar year, you can contribute for that year up to the date (without extensions) that you file your personal income tax return for that year. When you lose your HSA eligibility, you are no longer able to make contributions to your HSA. However, you can make contributions reflecting the months that you were HSA-eligible during your final year of eligibility. Example: You are HSA-eligible through June 30, 2016, then begin coverage under a non-HSA-qualified plan. You were HSA-eligible half the calendar year. If you were covered on a family contract, you could contribute 6/12 of the $6,750 annual contribution limit, or $3,375. You can contribute up to $3,375 any time before you file your 2016 personal income tax return, but no later than April 15, 2017. *IRS Notice 2008-59, Q&A 19.*

You do not declare a binding annual contribution election before the beginning of the year. Instead, you make contributions in any amount during the year up to your maximum contribution (statutory maximum annual contribution less any reductions based on your particular situation). This feature is very different from a Health FSA, which requires a fixed annual election that you cannot change as your needs change during the year. (Note: You can change a Health FSA election if you experience a life event such as marriage, divorce, birth, adoption, or death.)

You are not required to make level HSA contributions during the year. You can front-load, back-load, stagger contributions, or contribute in equal installments throughout the year, based on your cash flow, reimbursement needs, and preferences. You can make some or all of your contributions through a Cafeteria Plan (pre-tax payroll plan) if your employer offers this option, or you can make some or all of your contribution with personal (after-tax) funds that you subsequently deduct on your personal income tax return. *IRS Notice 2004-2, Q&A 21.*

You can have more than one HSA, but your maximum contribution does not change. Some individuals have more than one HSA for a variety of reasons. Your maximum contribution, though, is based on how many people your HSA-qualified plan covers and your age, not your number of active HSA accounts. Thus, you can contribute no more than the statutory maximum annual contribution, plus the $1,000 catch-up contribution if you are eligible, less any reductions that may apply to your particular situation (such as losing eligibility during the year or receiving non-preventive or non-service-connected care through a Department of Veterans Services facility). *IRS Notice 2004-2, Q&A 12.*

If both you and your spouse are HSA-eligible, enrolled on a family contract and have your own HSAs, you can contribute no more than the statutory maximum annual contribution. You can each contribute to your own HSA in any amount that you choose, as long as the sum of the contributions to the two HSAs does not exceed the statutory maximum annual contribution, less any reductions that apply to your particular situation. For many married couples, it makes sense for only one spouse to maintain an HSA, since accountholders often incur maintenance fees and either spouse's HSA can reimburse the other's expenses. The two-HSA approach may make sense if you prefer separate finances, have an HSA with a balance from your former employer's coverage or the spouse without an HSA is eligible to make a catch-up contribution (discussed below). *IRC Section 223 (b)(5) (b)(2)* and *IRS Notice 2004-50, Q&A 32.*

If both you and your spouse are HSA eligible and enrolled on two self-only contracts, you are treated as two separate individuals and can each contribute up to that year's individual maximum. In some years, like 2015, the total of two individual contributions may be higher than the family total. This situation occurs most often when two working spouses with no children find that it costs them less in premiums to purchase two individual contracts than to have family coverage. The IRS does not address this situation directly in it guidance, but many reliable sources corroborate that this is true, and I now agree that this more aggressive approach is acceptable. *IRS Notice 2008-59, Q&A 17*

If two or more individuals not married to each other are covered under one family contract, each can open his or her own HSA and contribute to the family maximum. This situation might occur if the health plan contract covers domestic partners or ex-spouses. It might also occur on a parent's contract that covers a child who is not a tax dependent of the parent but is permitted to remain under the parent's insurance contract as a result of the carrier's policy, state law, or provisions of the Affordable Care Act of 2010.

Neither the original legislation nor IRS interpretation to date has addressed this situation directly. Perhaps the safest strategy would be to ensure that the total contributions to all HSAs owned by individuals covered under the family contract not exceed the statutory maximum family contribution ($6,550 in 2014) with allowance for any individual eligible to make a catch-up contribution to deposit an additional $1,000 into his HSA.

Many HSA trustees and attorneys advise clients that they may wish to consider a more aggressive strategy. Since Section 223 and subsequent IRS notices are very specific in setting the rules for married couples (they are subject to the statutory maximum annual contribution to a family contract to be divided between the two in any percentage that they choose), these trustees and attorneys argue that this contribution limit does not apply to nonmarried, HSA-eligible individuals covered on a single family contract. They argue that since each individual is covered on a family contract and they are not married to each other, each individual can contribute up to the family contribution maximum.

CONTRIBUTION LIMITS AND INELIGIBLE INDIVIDUALS ON THE HEALTH INSURANCE CONTRACT

If you are covered on a family contract, you can contribute up the statutory maximum annual contribution for a family contract, even if no other family member is HSA-eligible. The contribution limit is driven by the type of insurance contract (self-only or family), not the number of HSA-eligible individuals on the contract. *IRS Notice 2008-59, Q&A 16.*

TAX BENEFITS

Contributions to your HSA, up to the annual limit, are deductible from your federal taxable income. You do not pay federal income or payroll taxes on contributions to your HSA. *IRC Section 223(a)* and *IRS Notice 2004-2, Q&A 17.*

Contributions to HSAs are deductible against most states' income taxes as well. Most states allow you to deduct your HSA contributions from state income taxes. The exceptions, as of September 2014, are Alabama, California, and New Jersey. In addition, in the states of Tennessee and New Hampshire, which do not have state income taxes, your account growth may be subject to state investment taxes. Check with your state, though, as state tax policy may change over time.

Anyone can contribute to your HSA. Your employer can deduct any contributions on its income tax return, which also reduces your taxable income. You can deduct contributions that you or anyone else (parent, spouse, neighbor) makes to your HSA. *IRS Notice 2004-2, Q&A 11.*

PRE-TAX PAYROLL CONTRIBUTIONS

If your employer offers a Cafeteria Plan, you can make pre-tax payroll contributions to an HSA. This is the best way to make contributions. Your entire contribution goes to work immediately in your HSA without any federal payroll, federal income, and state income (if applicable) taxes deducted. In addition, many people find it less painful to contribute in small chunks regularly to build a balance than it is not to contribute and then to incur a large expense without available HSA balances to cover the bill. *IRS Notice 2004-2, Q&A 33.*

Your employer reports these contributions in Box 12 of your annual W-2 earnings statements. Employer contributions and employee pre-tax payroll contributions are both considered employer contributions for W-2 reporting. *IRS Notice 2004-2, Q&A 19.*

You are allowed to make changes to your level of pre-tax payroll contributions. Your employer must allow you to make changes in your level of pre-tax contributions periodically (generally interpreted as at least monthly, consistent with the monthly determination of HSA eligibility). This flexibility to change your contribution stands in stark contrast to an FSA, where you are bound by an annual election unless you experience a qualifying event (such as birth, adoption, death, marriage, or divorce).

When you make pre-tax payroll deductions, you do not pay Social Security payroll taxes on these contributions. You save the 6.2% Social Security payroll tax and 1.45% Medicare payroll tax that you typically pay on taxable income. Your company saves the same amount, or if you are self-employed, you experience the full 15.3% savings. The IRS reports the lower income figure on which you pay payroll taxes to the Social Security Administration, which uses the figures to determine your initial Social Security monthly benefit. The lower figure may impact your future Social Security benefits, though the impact (if any) depends on your income level.

If you do not want to impact your future Social Security benefits, you can contribute personal funds and pay the applicable payroll taxes as you earn the money. Nothing prevents you from making post-tax payroll contributions and making personal (after-tax) HSA contributions. Example: You earn $50,000 per year. You can make your annual $5,000 HSA contribution through your employer's Cafeteria Plan (in which case you'll save $382.50 in payroll taxes but have only $45,000 in income reported to Social Security), or you can take your entire $50,000 as salary and then make a personal contribution to your HSA. In the latter scenario, you get back the income taxes that you paid on your $5,000 contribution, forfeit the savings of $382.50 in payroll taxes and have $50,000 of income reported to the Social Security Administration.

CONTRIBUTIONS AND PARTIAL-YEAR ELIGIBILITY

If you lose HSA eligibility during a calendar year, you must pro-rate your contributions. To pro-rate, you divide the number of months that you were HSA-eligible by twelve months, then multiply that fraction by the contribution that you were entitled to make if you did not lose your eligibility. For example, if you are under age fifty-five and covered on a self-only policy and you lose coverage effective July 1, 2016 (for example, by enrolling in Medicare or leaving your job without continuing your insurance), you would divide six months of coverage by twelve months (the fraction 6/12) and multiply that fraction by your statutory maximum annual contribution of $3,350 for a maximum contribution of $1,675. If you are age fifty-five or older, you also can pro-rate your $1,000 catch-up contribution (an additional $500), for a total contribution of $2,175. *IRC Section 223(b)(2)* and *IRS Notice 2004-2, Q&A 13.*

If you become HSA-eligible during the year and are eligible as of December 1, you can pro-rate or make a full contribution. If you pro-rate, you take the number of months that you are HSA-eligible and divide that figure by twelve, then multiply by the statutory maximum annual contribution for that year. If you are under age fifty-five, enroll on a family contract, become HSA-eligible April 1, 2016, and remain HSA-eligible the remainder of the year, you can contribute 9/12 of $6,750 or $5,062.50.

Alternatively, under the "last month" rule, you can make a full contribution for the year ($6,750, given the facts above) if you are HSA-eligible as of December 1 and remain HSA-eligible through the end of the *following* calendar year. In our example above, you need to remain HSA-eligible through December 31, 2017, to make the full contribution for 2016. If you fail to remain HSA-eligible through the "testing period" (which begins December 1, 2016, and extends through December 31, 2017, in the example above), you must include any contribution above the pro-rated amount in your taxable income and pay a 10% penalty. Unlike a normal excess contribution, you do not have to remove the contribution from your account and the interest or other gain does not figure into the penalty.

Here's an illustration of the financial impact of losing HSA eligibility during the Last Month rule testing period. Again, using the example above, you fail to renew your enrollment in an HSA-qualified plan April 1, 2017, after making a full $6,750 contribution for 2016. You must pro-rate your 2016 contribution ($6,750 that you contributed less the $5,062.50 pro-rated maximum equals an excess contribution of $1,687.50). You then include the $1,687.50 excess contribution in your 2017 taxable income and pay a 10% penalty ($168.75). Your net loss is really just $168.75, because that's your only additional actual cost above what you would have paid in taxes had you pro-rated your contribution. *IRC Section 223(b)(8)(B), IRS Notice 2004-2, Q&A 22 and Health Opportunity and Patient Empowerment Act of 2006, Section 5.*

You report your HSA activity, including excess contributions, on Form 8889 of your personal income tax return. Form 8889 guides you through the process of determining excess contributions and the associated adjustments to your taxable income and income tax liability. *IRS Form 8889.*

MISTAKEN AND EXCESS CONTRIBUTIONS

If you make contributions in excess of your annual maximum into your HSA, you can correct your mistake without an IRS penalty before filing your income tax return for that year. In this case, you need to remove any contribution above the amount that you were entitled to make for that calendar year and any earnings on those excess contributions and include that amount in that year's taxable income. As long as you do so, you are not subject to penalty. Your trustee may charge a fee for reversing these transactions. *IRC Section 223 (f)(3)(A), IRS Notice 2004-2, Q&A 22* and *IRS Notice 2004-50, Q&A 34.*

If you make excess contributions to your HSA and do not discover your error prior to filing your income tax return for that year, you can correct your mistake by reducing the following year's contribution by an equal amount. This strategy requires that you remain HSA-eligible during the following year, which often is not the case with individuals who make excess contributions. If you are in this position, you must pay a 6% excise tax on the excess contribution and reduce the second year's contribution so that the sum of the two years' contributions does not exceed the maximum contribution to which you were entitled during the two-year period. *Instructions for Form 8889, section entitled "Deducting an Excess Contribution in a Later Year," page 6 of the 2013 version of the form.*

If you keep an excess contribution in your HSA, you must include the excess amount as taxable income, pay a 6% excise tax and pay an annual 6% excise tax in perpetuity on all account gains associated with that excess contribution. This approach results in a bookkeeping nightmare. The first two options (removing the excess contribution before filing your personal income tax return for that year or reducing the following year's contribution by a like amount and paying the 6% excise tax on only that single year's excess contribution) are far easier to administer correctly. If you choose this option, you must file IRS Form 5329, *Additional Taxes on Qualified Plans (Including IRSAs) and Other Tax-Favored Accounts,* annually.

EMPLOYER CONTRIBUTIONS

Employers can make contributions into HSA-eligible employees' HSAs. Employers often make such contributions, especially during the first year or two of offering HSAs, and often when employees have a choice of enrolling in another plan.

An employer contribution, funded by the employer's premium savings, makes the HSA plan more attractive to you by lowering your net out-of-pocket financial responsibility and reflecting a partnership between you and your employer. *IRS Notice 2004-2, Q&A 12 and Q&A 19.*

Employers can allow employees to make pre-tax payroll contributions to their HSAs. Your employers must adopt a Cafeteria Plan (or file an amendment to their current Cafeteria Plan) to allow you and your co-workers to make pre-tax payroll contributions. Your contributions are deducted before federal and state (if applicable) income taxes and federal Social Security payroll taxes (both your employer's and your shares) are applied. Pre-tax payroll contributions are an excellent way to build HSA balances because you make regular deposits and the full value of your contribution goes to work immediately. *IRS Notice 2004-2, Q&A 33.*

If your employer allows you to make pre-tax payroll contributions, both employer and employee contributions are governed by Cafeteria Plan rules. Employer contributions are subject to either Cafeteria rules or comparability rules. Comparability rules, which are more rigid, apply only when an employer does not allow employees to make pre-tax payroll contributions. Most employers allow employees to make pre-tax payroll contributions both because (a) employees are more likely to contribute if they do so in small, regular increments and (b) employers do not have to pay their portion (6.2%) of payroll taxes on employees' salary deferrals through a Cafeteria Plan.

If your employer sets up a Cafeteria Plan, both employer and employee contributions are subject to Cafeteria Plan nondiscrimination rules. The IRS requires employers to test their Cafeteria Plans annually to ensure that highly-compensated employees do not benefit disproportionately relative to lower-paid workers. If the plan fails the testing, your employer must reduce highly-compensated employees' contributions through the Cafeteria Plan until the proportional benefit to highly-compensated employees is reduced enough to bring the plan back into balance. If you participate in a Cafeteria Plan that fails nondiscrimination testing, your employer may reduce your pre-tax payroll contribution below your annual maximum. Do not despair, though, as you can contribute the balance, up to your contribution maximum for the calendar year, with personal funds and deduct your personal contribution on your personal income tax return.

Employers can, under properly designed programs, offer matching employer HSA contributions or incentive payments through their Cafeteria Plan. Employers often provide matching programs to encourage employees to make contributions to their employer-sponsored qualified retirement plans such as a 401(k) or 403(b). HSA rules allow employers to design the same type of program for HSA contributions through a Cafeteria Plan. Also, employers can create incentive programs to encourage employees to complete a health risk assessment, undergo a routine physical, report certain biometric measurements (blood pressure and cholesterol levels are often the most common), or enroll in certain health-related programs to receive incentives. It is important for employers to design these programs in a manner that makes them nondiscriminatory (for example, by providing incentives based on completing an activity rather than achieving a specific outcome). Discrimination also can take the form of offering only an online written health risk assessment that a blind person cannot complete. *IRS Notice 2004-50, Q&A 47 and Q&A 49.*

Your employer can make negative elections into your HSA. A negative election is a contribution that the employer deducts automatically from your paycheck, without your explicit (positive) permission. For example, if the switch to an HSA-qualified plan saves employees on family coverage $40 per pay period, your employer can set up automatic pre-tax employee contributions of $40 per pay period through the company Cafeteria Plan. Your employer might surmise that you will not notice the difference (since there is no net reduction in your paycheck) and will appreciate the money in your HSA when you begin to incur expenses. You can choose to end the negative elections at any time by choosing to take a part or all of this HSA contribution out of the account in the form of cash, and your employer cannot interfere with your right to do so. Employers typically do not impose negative elections. *IRS Notice 2004-50, Q&A 61.*

If your employer does not set up a Cafeteria Plan, its contributions are governed by comparability rules. This situation is uncommon, since most employers encourage employees to make pre-tax payroll contributions, which can be done only through a Cafeteria plan. Under comparability rules, your employer can divide employees into no more than three classes (full-time, part-time and former) and must contribute to the HSAs of employees in each class comparably (same percentage of the deductible or same dollar figure). Employers do have the option to contribute disproportionately to lower-paid employees' HSAs, but otherwise, they do not have much flexibility. Employers cannot make matching or incentive contributions under comparability rules. *IRS Notice 2004-50, Q&A 46 and Q&A 48 and HOPE Act, Section 306.*

If your employer's contribution plan fails to satisfy comparability rules, you are held harmless, but your employer is assessed a 35% penalty on all contributions to employees' HSA that year. A failure to follow the complicated comparability rules results in a steep employer fine. *IRS Notice 2004-2, Q&A 32.*

Employer contributions to employees' HSAs are independent of employees' claims experience. Employers fund HSAs based on a schedule that applies to all employees. Contributions are not based on need (high claims) or used as a reward (low claims). *IRS Notice 2004-2, Q&A 30.*

Employers do not have to make their contributions in one lump-sum. Employers can structure the timing of their contribution schedule as they wish, provided that they outline their program in their Cafeteria Plan document and adhere to it. Since contributions vest immediately and employers cannot recover funds if an employee leaves employment midyear, some employers choose to contribute semi-annually, quarterly, monthly, or per pay period. These schedules generally are allowable as long as they are clearly documented and then administered correctly and consistently. *IRS Notice 2004-50, Q&A 21.*

Employer contributions to employees' HSAs vest immediately. Employers do not have the flexibility, as they do with employer contributions to qualified retirement plans, to establish a vesting schedule based on tenure with the company. As soon as a contribution hits an employee's HSA, that money belongs to the employee (similar to a paycheck). *IRS Notice 2004-50, Q&A 82.*

CONTRIBUTIONS AND CERTAIN BUSINESS OWNERS

If you are a member of a Limited Liability Company (LLC), partner in a partnership or a 2% or greater owner of a Subchapter S corporation, you cannot receive a tax-free contribution from the business. Under IRS rules, owners of these entities and some immediate family members cannot receive tax-free contributions from the business, though these owners can give tax-free contributions to their employees and deduct those employee contributions as a business expense. If you are an owner of one of these entities, you must contribute personal funds and deduct your contribution on your personal income tax return. This restriction applies regardless of how you are paid by the firm (even if you receive your income on a Form W-2). *See IRS Notice 2005-8 for additional guidance.*

If you are a member of an LLC, partner in a partnership or 2% or greater owners of a Subchapter S corporation, you cannot make pre-tax payroll contributions to your HSA. These owners are not eligible to participate in a Cafeteria Plan, the program that allows employees to elect to defer a portion of their salary as a nontaxable benefit. Since pre-tax payroll contributions can be made only through a Cafeteria Plan, these owners cannot make their HSA contributions on a pre-tax basis. Instead, they make personal contributions and deduct those contributions on their personal income tax forms.

This restriction impacts owners financially in two ways. First, because they receive their tax break when they file their personal income tax returns rather than when they contribute, they lose the use (including the potential investment value) of their tax deduction between the time of their contribution and their income tax filing. Second, they cannot recover federal payroll taxes paid on those contributions through their personal income tax filing. The full financial impact depends on whether their taxable income falls above (2.9% total levy) or below (15.3% total levy) the $118,500 taxable income ceiling for Social Security taxes in 2015.

If you own a Subchapter C corporation, you generally can receive a tax-free contribution from the business and make Cafeteria Plan pre-tax payroll contributions. Subchapter C owners usually are considered employees of the business entity. In these cases, they are treated the same as other employees with regard to HSA contributions.

TRACKING CONTRIBUTIONS

You are responsible for tracking contributions from all sources to ensure that they do not exceed the maximum contribution to which they are entitled in a calendar year. You manage your HSA. You are solely responsible for knowing the maximum contribution that you are entitled to make in a given calendar year. That figure may be less than the statutory maximum annual contribution based on the number of months that you are HSA-eligible. *IRS Notice 2004-50, Q&A 74.*

Your HSA trustee is responsible for setting its system to accept no more in contributions than the maximum annual contribution for a family contract, plus the $1,000 catch-up contribution if you represent your age as fifty-five or older. These restrictions are designed to protect the trustee, not you! Any number of circumstances may result in your not being able to contribute that amount into your HSA each year. Those circumstances range from being enrolled in a self-only contract to having received non-preventive or non-service-connected care through the VA or waiting for your spouse's Health FSA plan year to end. Your HSA trustee does not know about lower limits that apply to your situation. Some forward-looking trustees are beginning to promote tools, which make it easier for you to track this yourself via web or text alerts, but in most cases, they only prevent an over-contribution using the crude family plus one catch-up calculation noted above. *IRS Notice 2004-50, Q&A 73 and Q&A 75.*

If your employer allows you to contribute through pre-tax payroll, the employer is responsible for ensuring that you do not contribute more through pre-tax payroll than the statutory maximum for your contract type (self-only or family) and that you are not ineligible because you participate in the company's general Health FSA program. Your employer is not responsible for monitoring and stopping employee contributions based on disqualifying considerations outside the workplace that make you ineligible for any month or months during the calendar year (such as whether you are covered by your spouse's general Health FSA, receive ineligible care through a VA facility, or make personal contributions to an HSA). Your employer's sole responsibility is to determine that you have HSA-qualified coverage (and the level of coverage), you do not have any disqualifying coverage through the employer (such as a general Health FSA) and your age (to determine whether you can make a catch-up contribution because you're age fifty-five or older) to determine your maximum contribution through the company Cafeteria Plan. *IRS Notice 2004-50, Q&A 81.*

CONTRIBUTION LIMITS WHEN YOU HAVE MULTIPLE ACCOUNTS

You are bound by the statutory maximum annual contribution limits, regardless of how many HSAs you have. You may want to open more than one HSA if you follow one of several specific strategies discussed in Part 3 of this book. Regardless of how many HSAs you have or under how many HSA-qualified health insurance plans you are covered, your maximum contribution cannot exceed the statutory maximum annual contribution for your contract type (plus a $1,000 catch-up contribution if you are age fifty-five or older). *IRS Notice 2004-50, Q&A 64.*

If both you and your spouse have HSAs and are eligible to contribute, the sum of your contributions to the two accounts cannot exceed the maximum family contribution ($6,750 in 2016), plus a catch-up contribution into the HSA of whichever of you is entitled to make one. The law allows a husband and wife who are both HSA-eligible to split the applicable maximum family contract between their two HSAs as they choose. Catch-up contributions, though, must be deposited into the HSA of the individual who is eligible to make the catch-up contribution. *IRC Section 213(b)(5)(B)(ii)* and *IRS Notice 2004-50, Q&A 32.*

If you are HSA-eligible and covered by a Post-Deductible (or the rare Limited-Purpose) HRA, your HRA does not affect your ability to make the full HSA contribution to which you are otherwise entitled. You can be covered on a family HSA-qualified insurance plan with a $10,000 deductible and an employer-funded HRA that reimburses all expenses once you reach $2,600 (2016 figure). In that case, you can still make the statutory maximum annual contribution for a family contract (less any reductions specific to your situation).

IRS Notice 2004-50, Q&A 33 and *Revenue Ruling 2004-045, Situations 2 and 4.*

If you make an election into a Limited-Purpose (or the rare Post-Deductible) Health FSA, that election does not affect your ability to make a full HSA contribution to which you are otherwise entitled. You can reduce your taxable income by making an election into a Limited-Purpose Health FSA that reimburses eligible dental, vision, and preventive care services only. Your maximum contribution for a health FSA of any type is determined by your employer, not to exceed $2,600 (2016 figure). *Revenue Ruling 2004-045, Situations 2 and 4*

Reporting Contributions

You are responsible for accurately reporting contributions on your personal income tax return. Because an HSA is an individual account, you (not your employer or HSA trustee) are responsible for reporting account activity to the IRS. Your employer and your trustee will provide you with some information for your personal reporting and recordkeeping, but you alone are responsible for reporting your activity accurately. *IRS Notice 2004-50, Q&A 74*

If you make pre-tax payroll contributions through your employer's Cafeteria Plan, those contributions will be reflected on your W-2, which your employer issues by January 31. For tax purposes, both employer and employee contributions through a Cafeteria Plan are labeled as employer contributions. They appear as a total in Box 12 of your Form W-2. Box 12 is a catch-all that holds information about a variety of pre-tax programs that your employer offers. Your HSA contributions are included in Box 12 with the code "W." *IRS Publication "2012 General Instructions for Form W-2 and W-3," p. 17*

Your trustee issues Form 5498-SA by May 31 each year. This form indicates contributions made the previous calendar year and the account value as of that date. Trustees are not required to issue Form 5498-SA until May 31 because you can contribute up to the date that you file your personal income tax return (without extensions). Some HSA trustees will issue the 5498-SA in January and then issue a revised form in May if you have further activity. Most HSA trustees will report your YTD total contributions on their website, via online search tool or via phone. *IRS Publication "Instructions for Form 1099-SA and Form 5498-SA."*

You report your HSA contributions on Form 1040 (page 1) and on Form 8889 of your personal income tax return. You receive the deduction whether you file Form 1040 (Long Form), Form 1040A (Short Form) or Form 1040 EZ.

EXCESS CONTRIBUTIONS

The sum of your contributions that exceeds your applicable maximum contribution in a given year is considered an excess contribution. You are responsible for managing contributions to your HSA. You may at some point make contributions in excess of your allowed amount. This situation occurs most often when you front-load your contribution and then lose eligibility during the year. *IRS Notice 2004-2, Q&A 22.*

You can avoid penalties by removing the excess contributions, and any account earnings attributable to the excess earnings, before filing your income taxes for that year. This is by far the easiest and least expensive approach to addressing this issue. Example: You are entitled to contribute $3,350 (self-only contract maximum contribution for 2016). You make a full lump-sum contribution in January 2016. You lose your HSA eligibility September 9, leaving you with only nine months of eligibility and thus a maximum contribution of only $2,512.50. You can remove the additional $837.50 and any earnings on that amount (which probably is less than $2 in the current interest-rate environment) no later than six months after the due date (without extensions) of your 2016 income tax return and include that amount in your 2016 taxable income. Your HSA trustee will usually help you execute this transaction correctly, but may charge a special fee to do the reversal transaction. See IRS Form 5329 instructions, Lines 43 and 47, for more information. *IRC Section 223(f)(3)(A), IRS Form 5329 Instructions, Line 47, IRS Notice 2004-2, Q&A 22* and *IRS Notice 2004-50, Q&A 34.*

If you make excess contributions through your employer's Cafeteria Plan, you need to work with your employer to adjust your W-2. Pre-tax payroll contributions flow through your employer's Cafeteria Plan. If you made excess contributions through the Cafeteria Plan, you need to withdraw the excess contribution and any earnings on it (as outlined above) and have your employer adjust your W-2 to reflect the proper contribution. It is best to inform your employer before the end of the calendar year. Otherwise, your employer may have to issue a revised W-2, which increases administrative work and may delay your completing your personal income tax return.

You can correct your excess contribution by reducing the following year's contribution by the amount of this year's excess contribution. If you do not catch your error in time, you can bring your account back in compliance by calculating your excess contribution in 2016 (plus the earnings on the excess contribution), paying a 6% excise tax (by completing Form 5329) on that amount on your 2016 personal income tax return and reducing your 2017 maximum contribution by an equal amount. This option is available only if you remain HSA-eligible during enough of the year following the excess contribution to absorb the excess contribution.

If you do not correct your excess contribution, you must pay a 6% excise tax on the excess contribution and a 6% excise tax every year on the account gains associated with that excess contribution. This approach becomes very cumbersome for your annual personal income tax filings. You need to calculate the excise tax on the initial excess contribution and then annually on the account growth attributable to the excess contribution. You must file Form 5329 annually. *IRS Notice 2004-2, Q&A 22.*

EMPLOYER CONTRIBUTIONS

Your employer can contribute to your HSA. Employers often make contributions to employees' HSAs, particularly in the first few years of the program, to help employees build account balances. Employers can deduct these contributions on their tax returns.

Your employer determines the timing of the employer contribution. Employers can decide whether they want to make annual, semi-annual, quarterly, or monthly contributions, or make contributions per pay period. The timing and amounts are spelled out in the HSA amendment to your employer's Cafeteria Plan. In determining the amount and timing of contributions, employers typically weigh what they can afford to give that year, their cash flow and how much they want to help employees with the new plan (or how much they want to encourage employees with health plan options to choose the HSA plan.

Employer contributions are applied to your contribution maximum. Your maximum contribution (the statutory maximum annual contribution for your contract type, less any downward adjustments if you were not HSA-eligible one or more months) includes deposits from all sources. Typically, you and your employer are the sources of contributions, but anyone else can contribute to your HSA, and as you'll learn later, you can make a one-time rollover from an IRA to an HSA. The cumulative total contribution from all these sources must not exceed the maximum contribution to which you are entitled in a given calendar year. *IRS Notice 2004-2, Q&A 12.*

Employer contributions vest immediately in nearly all cases. When your employer places money in your HSA, it travels in only one direction—into your account. Your employer cannot recoup any of the money if, for example, you leave employment the following week or lose your HSA eligibility the following month when you enroll in Medicare Part A. *IRS Notice 2008-59, Q&A 25*

Your employer can recoup contributions if you were never HSA-eligible. This situation is the rare exception to the rule that employer contributions vest immediately. The reason for the exception: You were never HSA-eligible and therefore could not legally establish the account into which the employer made the contribution. Note, however, if you were HSA-eligible at one time during the year and your employer made an additional contribution after you lost your HSA eligibility, your employer cannot recoup that money (though you must include it in your taxable income, since it amounts to taxable compensation if you are no longer HSA-eligible). *IRS Notice 2008-59, Q&A 23.*

If your employer attempts to recoup a contribution because you were never HSA-eligible, your trustee does not have to return the money. Most trustees work with the employer, particularly when the employer has forged a relationship with that trustee to provide HSA trustee services to employees. If the trustee does not return the money to your employer, your employer cannot force you to return the money. Instead, the employer can include the amount of the contribution as taxable income on your W-2. *IRS Notice 2008-59, Q&A 23.*

Your employer can make a contribution into your spouse's HSA. This situation occurs most often either when (1) you are no longer HSA-eligible, but your spouse remains on the group plan and is HSA-eligible or (2) you enroll on your spouse's plan and your employer shares some of its premium savings with you. This contribution is not done on a pre-tax basis. Instead, it is taxable as income to you at the time of receipt, but your spouse can deduct the contribution on his or her (or your joint) federal income tax return. *IRS Notice 2008-59, Q&A 26.*

KEY POINTS IN THIS CHAPTER

- The IRS sets the maximum annual contribution based on contract type and may revise it each year. The maximum includes contributions from all sources, including your employer.

- You and any other HSA-eligible person on your contract (such as your spouse) can contribute an additional $1,000 annually beginning at age fifty-five.

- If you are covered on a family contract, you can contribute up to the applicable maximum family contribution, even if you are the only HSA-eligible individual on your health insurance contract.

- You can make pre-tax payroll contributions if your employer offers a Cafeteria Plan.

- You can make personal (after-tax) contributions to your HSA. You deduct these contributions from your taxable income on your personal income tax return.

- You can make personal contributions whether or not your employer offers pre-tax contributions through a Cafeteria Plan (though, in most cases, you enjoy additional tax advantages by contributing through a Cafeteria Plan). If your employer doesn't offer a Cafeteria plan, you're self-employed, or you're an owner of certain business entities, your only option is to make personal contributions directly to the trustee.

- You determine the amount and timing of your HSA contributions. You do not make a binding annual election through your employer's Cafeteria Plan.

- Married couples who are both HSA-eligible can split the family contribution as they wish.

- The IRS has not ruled on the maximum contribution and division requirements for domestic partners, though many attorneys and trustees are advising their clients that each domestic partner may be eligible to make contributions up to the statutory maximum for a family contract.

- Contributions are either pre-tax or deductible at the federal level. Several states assess income taxes on contributions or investment taxes on account earnings.
- If you lose your HSA eligibility midyear, you must pro-rate your contributions based on the number of months that you were HSA-eligible.
- If you become HSA-eligible after January 1 but no later than December 1, you can either pro-rate your contribution or make a full contribution, provided that you remain HSA-eligible through December 31 of the *following* year.
- If you contribute too much to your HSA, you can correct your error before filing your taxes or incur penalties.

Consumer Checklist

✓ Learn before the beginning of the plan year the amount and timing of your employer contribution so that you can plan your personal contributions accordingly.

✓ Plan to make pre-tax payroll contributions if your employer offers a Cafeteria Plan. You should begin the discipline of regular HSA deposits.

✓ Check to see whether your employer already has set up a negative election. Most do not, but some do.

✓ Review your contributions before the end of the calendar year to make sure that you have not made an excess contribution (and correct the excess contribution if you have made one).

✓ If you are looking for sources of funds to contribute through a Cafeteria Plan and plan to use a portion of your HSA as a long-term savings and investment vehicle, consider adopting HSA Strategy 5 (discussed later in this book).

TEST YOUR KNOWLEDGE

1. **You cover your spouse (age sixty-seven) and yourself (age fifty-nine) on your HSA-qualified plan. Your spouse is enrolled in Medicare. How much can you contribute in 2016?**

    A. Up to the statutory maximum for a self-only contract, since you are the only HSA-eligible person on the contract.

    B. Up to the statutory maximum for a family contract, plus a catch-up contribution for you.

    C. You cannot contribute since your spouse's enrollment in Medicare disqualifies you both from contributing.

    D. Up to the statutory maximum for a family contract; plus each of you can make a catch-up contribution into your individual HSAs.

2. **You commit to contributing $50 per pay period to your HSA. Midyear, you realize that you need to contribute more. What can you do?**

    A. You can change your election or contribute personal funds that you can deduct when you file your income taxes.

    B. You are locked into your annual contribution, so your only option is to contribute personal funds and take a tax deduction.

    C. You cannot change your election or contribute personal funds.

    D. You cannot change your election, but you can discontinue your pre-tax payroll contributions and deposit tax-deductible personal funds.

3. **You (age fifty-six) and your wife (age fifty-five) are covered on your policy, and both of you open HSAs. What's your maximum contribution to each HSA in 2016?**

   A. You can each fund your own HSA up to the self-only contribution limit, plus you can make a catch-up contribution into your HSA.

   B. You must make equal contributions into each HSA, plus you can make a catch-up contribution into your HSA.

   C. You must make equal contributions and must factor your catch-up contribution into that calculation.

   D. You can divide the maximum family contribution between the two HSAs as you choose, plus you can each make a catch-up contribution into your individually owned HSAs.

4. **You are enrolled on a self-only contract and become HSA-eligible May 1, 2016. How much can you contribute to your HSA in 2016?**

   A. Your contribution is limited to 8/12 of the statutory maximum annual contribution for your contract type.

   B. You cannot contribute more than 8/12 of your deductible.

   C. You cannot contribute this year.

   D. You can contribute 8/12 of the statutory maximum contribution or up to the full maximum contribution if you remain eligible through the "testing period."

5. **You are a partner in a law practice. You are enrolled in an HSA-qualified plan and meet HSA eligibility criteria. Which of the following statements is true?**

   A. You can make a personal tax-deductible contribution to your HSA.

B. You cannot contribute because you are an owner.

C. You cannot deduct your contributions.

D. If you draw a salary from the firm, you can contribute up to the maximum for your contract type through pre-tax payroll deduction.

6. **You are enrolled on a self-only contract and lose your HSA eligibility as of August 1 when you enroll in Medicare on your sixty-fifth birthday. How much can you contribute in 2016?**

A. Up to 7/12 of the statutory maximum contribution, plus 7/12 of the catch-up contribution.

B. Up to 7/12 of the statutory maximum contribution, but no catch-up contribution.

C. Up to the maximum contribution, plus the full catch-up, as long as you were HSA-eligible during the past three years.

D. Up to 7/12 of the statutory maximum contribution, plus the full catch-up contribution.

7. **Your employer offers an additional HSA contribution as an incentive to join a gym. What can you conclude about the incentive contribution?**

A. It is subject to Cafeteria Plan nondiscrimination testing.

B. It is subject to comparability rules.

C. It is not legal and could disqualify you from being HSA-eligible.

D. It is not legal and can result in a 20% penalty to the employer, but the IRS would hold you harmless because you did not make the mistake.

8. **Your daughter enrolls in an HSA-eligible plan when she accepts her first full-time job. You want to reward her by making a $2,000 contribution to her HSA. What is the impact of that contribution?**

   A. You cannot contribute to anyone's HSA unless you are HSA-eligible.

   B. You can make the contribution, which offsets what she herself can contribute, and she receives the tax deduction.

   C. You can contribute to her HSA and take a tax deduction.

   D. You can contribute, and as long as you are HSA-eligible and reduce your contribution to your HSA by an equal amount, she can make a full contribution to her HSA.

9. **You begin to prepare your income tax return and realize that you did not fully fund last year's HSA. Can you remedy this problem now?**

   A. No. Your deadline for contributions is December 31.

   B. Yes. You can contribute personal funds or ask your employer to make pre-tax payroll deductions to increase last year's contribution.

   C. No. Your deadline for contributions is January 31, when you receive your Form 1099-SA.

   D. Yes. You can contribute personal funds and take a tax deduction up to the date that you file that year's income tax return (without extensions).

10. **You open two HSAs in your name. What impact does owning two HSAs have on your contribution limit?**

A. You cannot contribute to more than one in any given year.

B. You can contribute to either or both in any proportion that you want, as long as you do not exceed the statutory annual maximum for your contract.

C. You can contribute to both, but only in equal amounts.

D. You can contribute to only one, unless you are entitled to make a catch-up contribution, in which case you can make the catch-up contribution into the second HSA.

Test Your Knowledge Answers

1. B. You are covered under a family contract, so you can contribute up to the family maximum, even if no one else covered under the contract is HSA-eligible. You can make a catch-up contribution because you are age fifty-five or older and HSA-eligible. Your spouse, who is not HSA-eligible, cannot make a catch-up contribution.

2. A. You are not locked into an annual HSA contribution (as you are with a Health FSA, except for certain qualifying events). Your employer must allow you to change your pre-tax payroll deductions, and you always have the flexibility to make a personal contribution and deduct it when you file your personal income tax return for that year.

3. D. You can split the statutory maximum annual contribution for a family contract between the two HSAs as you see fit. Catch-up contributions must be made into the HSA of the person who's eligible to make the contribution.

4. D. You have the choice of pro-rating your contribution or following the "last-month" rule, in which case you can contribute up to the statutory maximum annual contribution for your contract type, provided that you remain HSA-eligible through December 31 of the following calendar year.

5. A. You can make a full contribution. Because you are an owner, however, you cannot participate in a Cafeteria Plan, the program that allows employees to make pre-tax payroll contributions.

6. A. You must pro-rate your regular and catch-up contribution because you lose HSA eligibility during the year.

7. A. Such incentive contributions are permitted only through a Cafeteria Plan.

8. B. Anyone can contribute to an HSA-eligible individual's account. The accountholder receives the tax deduction.

9. D. You can make personal contributions up to the time that you file your personal income tax return. You cannot make pre-tax payroll contributions after the close of the calendar year to which the contributions are credited.

10. B. Your maximum contribution cannot exceed the statutory maximum annual contribution for your contract type. You can allocate the allowable contribution between the two accounts as you see fit.

HSA Distributions
(Withdrawals)

Distributions from a Health Savings Account are tax free as long as they are eligible expenses, are incurred by individuals eligible for tax-free distributions from your HSA, and are incurred during an eligible time period. You must include in your taxable income, in the year of distribution, all withdrawals that do not meet these criteria. In addition, you are responsible for an additional 20% tax if you are under age sixty-five and not disabled. *IRS Notice 2004-2, Q&A 25.*

You do not have to be HSA-eligible any longer to make tax-free distributions from your HSAs. HSA eligibility impacts only your ability to establish and contribute to the HSA, not to make qualified tax-free withdrawals. You can reimburse eligible expenses tax-free from your HSA at any point in the future after you establish your HSA, as long as you have balances remaining in your HSA. *IRC Section 223(f)(1)* and *IRS Notice 2004-2, Q&A 28.*

Eligible Time Period

You can reimburse eligible expenses tax-free as long as you incur the expenses on or after the date that you "establish" your HSA. While you become HSA-eligible as of the date that you enroll in an HSA-qualified plan and do not have any disqualifying coverage or other situations, you do not begin to enjoy tax-free distributions until you "establish" your HSA by funding it. Your HSA generally is not established as of the effective date of your health plan. Rather, you follow applicable state trust laws to establish your HSA. *IRS Notice 2008-59, Q&A 38 and Q&A 39.*

The criteria for "establishing" an HSA are set by the laws of the state that has jurisdiction over the accounts. The IRS defers to state trust laws to determine when an HSA is "established." This date is important because you cannot reimburse any expenses that you incur before you legally establish your HSA. Many states require that you signal intent to open the trust, name a trust beneficiary and place something of value into the HSA.

Under this interpretation, an HSA is not established until your HSA receives an initial contribution, thereby limiting your tax-free reimbursements to expenses incurred after the date of your initial deposit. Be sure to take into consideration the timing of your employer's contribution or your employer's date of deposit of your pre-tax Cafeteria Plan payroll contributions. If your employer doesn't make the initial deposits until the first week after the first month of payroll deductions, you won't be able to reimburse tax-free any eligible expenses that you incur during the first five weeks of your HSA eligibility.

Trust laws vary by state. Utah passed an HSA-specific law in 2009 that allows accountholders to establish an HSA back to the date that they initially became HSA-eligible, as long as they makes a contribution to the HSA before filing tax returns for that tax (calendar) year. Under this law, you could become HSA-eligible January 1, delay opening your account, incur thousands of dollars of eligible expenses, make an initial HSA contribution by April 15 of the following year and subsequently make additional contributions to reimburse yourself tax free for all expenses incurred since you became HSA-eligible. Even if you do not live in Utah, this flexible standard may apply to your HSA if your trustee is domiciled in Utah and Utah law governs your HSA. (Two of the largest HSA trustees in America are based in Utah, so you might be pleasantly surprised.)

Some HSA trustees and custodians place a penny in the account on the first day of eligibility to establish accounts automatically (they use a transaction code that does not count toward the maximum contribution so that it does not interfere with other funding you must track). Others allow accountholders to reimburse tax-free any eligible expenses incurred after the accountholders become HSA-eligible but before they make an initial contribution if that gap is small (say, a week or a month), though there is no provision in the tax code or IRS interpretation explicitly supporting this practice. *IRS Notice 2008-59, Q&A 38 and Q&A 39.*

You do not have to reimburse an expense at the time that you incur it. You have great flexibility in determining when you reimburse an expense. As long as you retain receipts, you can reimburse an expense tax-free years (even decades) in the future. Of course, if you want to reimburse an expense immediately and enjoy the tax savings now, you can do so. On the other hand, if you want to build your HSA balance for future expenses (including eligible expenses in retirement, when your income may be lower), you can pay for eligible expenses with personal (after-tax) funds and allow your HSA balances to grow. At any point in the future, you can reimburse today's expenses. And you can mix-and-match, paying some current expenses with HSA funds (perhaps a large bill that you cannot pay easily with personal funds) and paying others with personal funds (perhaps smaller bills, so that you can build your balances for future large expenses). *IRS Notice 2004-2, Q&A 24.*

INDIVIDUALS WHOSE EXPENSES ARE/ ARE NOT ELIGIBLE FOR TAX-FREE DISTRIBUTION

An individual does not have to be HSA-eligible for you to reimburse his expenses tax-free from your HSA. Do not confuse the term "individual whose expenses are eligible for tax-free distribution" with "HSA-eligible individual." Expenses incurred by an individual are eligible for tax-free distribution from your HSA based on that individual's relationship to you, regardless of whether the individual himself is HSA-eligible. If the individual who incurs the expense is your spouse or tax dependent at the time the expense is incurred, you can reimburse his or her expenses tax-free from your HSA. *IRC Section 223(d)(2)(A).*

You can reimburse your own, your spouse's, and your dependents' eligible expenses. It does not matter whether these individuals are HSA-eligible, or whether they are covered under your insurance policy. As long as they have the legal relationship with you when the expense is incurred, their expenses can be reimbursed on a tax-free basis. Note: Section 152 of the IRC defines a dependent. *IRC Section 223(d)(1), IRC Section 223(d) (2)(A)* and *IRS Notice 2004-50, Q&A 36.*

You ordinarily cannot reimburse tax-free eligible expenses incurred by your domestic partner (same-sex or opposite sex). This partner does not meet the federal definition of spouse. You cannot reimburse his or her expenses unless the partner's expenses are eligible by another provision of tax law, such as the partner qualifies as your tax dependent (for example, due to disability as defined by Section 1811 of the Social Security Act).

You cannot reimburse an ex-spouse's expenses or expenses incurred by a legally separated spouse tax-free. This provision holds true even if you are required by court order to cover your ex-spouse on your insurance policy.

You cannot reimburse your child's expenses if that child does not qualify as your tax dependent. PPACA allows individuals to cover children on their health plan until the child's twenty-sixth birthday. Irrespective of this coverage, you cannot reimburse your child's expense if your child does not meet the Section 152 definition of a dependent at the time the expense is incurred. The only exception to this rule is for children of divorced parents who can have expenses paid by both parents in certain circumstances, even though only one parent may have legal custody. (See HSA Situations - HSAs and Divorce for more details.)

ELIGIBLE EXPENSES

There is no authoritative list of HSA-eligible expenses. The closest the IRS comes to such a list is *IRS Publication 502*, issued annually, which details the expenses eligible for the medical expense income tax deduction. This list of expenses eligible for the deduction is nearly identical to the list of HSA-eligible expenses. Beware, though, while *Publication 502* lists health insurance premiums as eligible expenses, they are eligible for tax-free distribution from an HSA only under limited circumstances. Most HSA trustees publish a list of HSA-eligible expenses derived from *Publication 502*, with appropriate adjustments relevant to HSAs. Such a list can be found at the HSA education site I run, AskMrHSA.com.

As a rule of thumb, any expense that diagnoses or treats an illness, injury, or condition is eligible for tax-free distribution from an HSA. This summary is the gist of Section 213(d). If you've participated in a Health FSA program, you know that you can reimburse "Section 213(d) expenses." Unfortunately, Section 213(d) does not provide a clean, succinct list of eligible services (*Publication 502* provides such a list and description). Section 213(d) essentially says that if a product or service diagnoses or treats an injury, illness, or condition, it is eligible for tax-favored treatment. The expense may be eligible for the medical income tax deduction, reimbursement from a Health FSA or HRA, or tax-free distribution from an HSA. *IRC Section 213(d)(2)(a)* and *IRS Notice 2004-2, Q&A 26.*

Health insurance premiums are an HSA-eligible expense only in certain circumstances. You can reimburse health insurance premiums tax-free from your HSA only if an individual is collecting public unemployment benefits or continuing coverage under provisions of the Consolidated Omnibus and Budget Reconciliation Act of 1986 (COBRA). If you subsequently no longer receive unemployment benefits or lose COBRA continuation rights, you no longer can reimburse health insurance premiums tax-free. *IRC Section 223(d)(2)(C)* and *IRS Notice 2004-2, Q&A 27.*

Medicare premiums are an eligible expense but only if the accountholder has turned age sixty-five. If you are not yet sixty-five, you cannot reimburse your own or your spouse's (or dependent's) Medicare premiums. You can reimburse all of your spouse's eligible expenses, including Medicare cost sharing (deductibles and coinsurance). *IRC Section 223(d)(2)(C)(iv), IRS Notice 2004-2, Q&A 27* and *IRS Notice 2004-50, Q&A 45.*

Premiums paid for a qualified long-term care insurance policy are an eligible expense. You can pay for long-term care insurance premiums tax-free from your HSA, regardless of your age, subject to limits, as long as the policy meets IRS qualification standards. The amount of premiums that you can reimburse varies with your age. The policy itself must meet IRS guidelines, including guaranteed renewability, no cash surrender value, and restrictions on refunds and dividends. *IRS Publication 502, published annually.*

MISTAKEN DISTRIBUTIONS

If you make a distribution from your HSA in error, you are permitted to return the funds. Mistaken distributions sometimes happen. You pull out the wrong debit card at the convenience store. You reimburse a provider for a claim that the insurer later reprocesses with no financial liability to you. Regardless of the situation, you are permitted to correct an honest mistake by contacting your HSA trustee and following its process for reversing a mistaken distribution. *IRS Notice 2004-50, Q&A 37.*

Your trustee is not required to accept repayment of mistaken distributions. The law does not require trustees to accept repayments in order not to create an administrative burden on trustees. In most cases, though, trustees have developed simple processes to allow you to replace any funds that you distributed by accident. After all, it is in the trustee's interest to maximize assets under management. *IRS Notice 2004-50, Q&A 76.*

TRUSTEE RESTRICTIONS ON DISTRIBUTIONS

Trustees cannot restrict your distributions to eligible expenses. Neither your trustee nor your employer can alter a basic HSA trust agreement to restrict your distributions to HSA-eligible expenses. You are permitted to make withdrawals at any time for any purpose, subject to taxes and penalties for expenses that are not HSA-eligible. *IRS Notice 2004-50, Q&A 79.*

Trustees can place reasonable restrictions on the frequency or amount of distributions. Again, while the law allows trustees to place these restrictions, few do. Trustees realize that theirs is a competitive market and that you have many other trustee options. They are generally designed to prevent fraud in the cases they are applied. These terms are spelled out in your trust agreement. *IRS Notice 2004-50, Q&A 80.*

If your trustee's HSA debit card restricts acceptance by merchant code, your trustee must provide an alternate means of making distributions. Health FSA administrators code their cards to restrict their acceptance to certain locations likely to offer eligible goods and services (such as dentists, optical shops, hospitals, labs, pharmacies, and physician offices). Health FSA cards also are coded to accept only certain over-the-counter items (eligible equipment and supplies) and to reject others. HSA trustees usually do not place such restrictions on HSA debit cards for two reasons. First, you are allowed to make withdrawals for any item, whether or not it is HSA-eligible (subject to penalties and taxes if the item is not HSA-eligible). Second, most trustees are banks and similar financial institutions, not Health FSA administrators. These institutions offer unrestricted debit and credit cards in other lines of business, and they typically do not invest in the more restrictive software when not required to do so. If your HSA trustee does restrict the debit card to HSA-eligible expenses or to merchants likely to offer eligible items and services, the trustee must provide you with another means to access your money. Typical alternatives (many of which are offered even with unrestricted cards) include a checkbook, a process to request a check (commonly referred to as "Online Bill Pay"), or a procedure to link your personal financial account to your HSA and move money as you wish between the accounts.

KEY POINTS IN THIS CHAPTER

- You do not have to be HSA-eligible to make tax-free distributions from your HSA.
- You do not have to reimburse an expense in the year that you incur it. You can defer reimbursement for years.
- You can make tax-free distributions for other individuals' eligible expenses, as long as those individuals meet the federal tax code definition of your spouse or your tax dependent at the time the expense is incurred.
- You cannot reimburse tax-free expenses incurred by individuals covered on your insurance policy if they are not your legal spouse or tax dependents.
- Family members do not have to be HSA-eligible themselves or covered on your health insurance plan for you to reimburse their eligible expenses tax-free from your HSA.

- You can make tax-free distributions to reimburse any expense that you incur after you establish your HSA. The date that you establish your HSA varies according to the state law that governs your HSA, so be sure to check with your HSA trustee.
- You cannot make a tax-free payment for your own or an eligible family member's Medicare premiums until you turn age sixty-five. You can, however, reimburse tax-free other eligible expenses incurred by a qualified family member enrolled in Medicare.
- Be sure to keep receipts. You'll need them in case you are audited. Furthermore, if you are preserving your HSA balance for future use (such as in retirement), keeping your receipts for unreimbursed eligible expenses allows you to make a large distribution to meet a sudden financial emergency (or if you want to buy a boat) without tax consequences so long as you can offset the distributions with unreimbursed eligible expenses.

Consumer Checklist

✓ Make sure you understand the rules surrounding tax-free distributions. *IRS Publication 502*, published annually, provides information on whose expenses and which expenses you can reimburse tax-free.

✓ Be sure to save your receipts. You will not submit them when you file your personal income tax return, but you'll need them later to document distributions for eligible expenses if the IRS audits your personal tax return.

✓ Even if you are a "saver" with no intention of reimbursing expenses prior to retirement, be sure to save receipts for all eligible expenses that you did not reimburse. If you face a future financial emergency (or just want to buy something cool or go somewhere warm) and need to raid your HSA for funds, you can match up distributions with these receipts and owe no taxes or penalties.

TEST YOUR KNOWLEDGE

1. **You do not reimburse an eligible expense in the year that you incur it. Which statement is true?**
    A. You can reimburse it tax-free in the future.
    B. You can reimburse it tax-free up to the time that you file your personal income tax return for that year.
    C. You lose your ability to reimburse it from your HSA.
    D. You can reimburse it in the future, but the distribution will not be tax-free.

2. **You reimburse an expense subject to the deductible under your health plan. You appeal the charge, and your insurer adjusts the claim to cover the expense in full. What is true of your distribution for that expense?**
    A. Since you made the distribution already, you must include it in your taxable income and pay a penalty.
    B. The reimbursement remains tax-free, since you made it before the insurer adjusted the claim.
    C. You can request that your HSA trustee accept the money back from you as a mistaken distribution, or the distribution is subject to taxes and penalties.
    D. You must report the distribution as taxable income, but the 20% penalty is waived because you did not know at the time of distribution that the claim would be adjusted.

3. **You retire at age sixty with a disability and become eligible for and enroll in Medicare immediately. What is true of your eligible expenses going forward?**

    A. You cannot reimburse any eligible expenses tax-free until you turn age sixty-five and would have qualified for Medicare without your disability.

    B. You can reimburse all eligible expenses tax-free only prior to turning age sixty-five.

    C. You can reimburse all eligible expenses tax-free except Medicare premiums, which are not eligible for tax-free distribution until you turn age sixty-five.

    D. You can reimburse all eligible expenses, including Medicare premiums, tax-free because the restriction on not reimbursing Medicare premiums until age sixty-five does not apply in the case of the accountholder's disability.

4. **Your spouse and children are not covered on your health plan. Which statement is true about distributions from your HSA to reimburse their eligible expenses?**

    A. Distributions are tax-free as long as they remain tax-dependents.

    B. Distributions are subject to income tax but not the 20% penalty.

    C. You cannot make tax-free distributions for their expenses because they are not covered on your health plan.

    D. Distributions are subject to income tax and a 20% penalty.

5. **You are age seventy and enrolled in Medicare, so you are no longer HSA-eligible. Which statement is true of your future distributions?**

    A. You can make distributions for any expense, whether eligible or not, but distributions for eligible expenses are subject to income tax and penalties.

    B. Distributions that you make for eligible expenses are subject to income tax but not penalties.

    C. You can make distributions for any expenses, whether eligible or not, but distributions for ineligible expenses are subject to income tax, but not penalties.

    D. All distributions are tax-free once you turn age sixty-five.

6. **Your domestic partner, who is not your tax dependent, incurs an eligible expense. Can you reimburse it from your HSA?**

    A. No, you cannot reimburse the expense tax-free from your HSA unless your domestic partner is a tax dependent (such as due to disability).

    B. Yes, you can reimburse the expense tax-free as long as your domestic partner is covered on your health plan.

    C. Yes, you can reimburse the expense tax-free if the domestic partner is of the same sex in a state that doesn't recognize same-sex marriage.

    D. Yes. You can reimburse the expense from your HSA, and the distribution will be taxed but not subject to a 20% penalty.

7. **You and your spouse both have HSAs with substantial balances. She incurs an eligible expense. Which statement is true?**

   A. You can reimburse her expense from your HSA, but it is subject to income tax and a 20% penalty.
   B. You cannot reimburse her expense tax-free from your HSA if she has HSA balances available to reimburse from her HSA.
   C. Either you or she can reimburse the expense tax-free from your respective HSAs.
   D. Neither of you can reimburse more than half the expense each from your respective HSAs.

TEST YOUR KNOWLEDGE ANSWERS

1. A. You face no time limits for making tax-free distributions from your HSA for eligible expenses.
2. C. You have an opportunity to work with your trustee to reverse the distribution with no tax implications or penalties. If you do not do so, the distribution is subject to taxes, plus a 20% penalty if you are under age sixty-five.
3. C. You can reimburse tax-free all eligible expenses that you incur for the rest of your life, though you cannot reimburse your own or anyone else's Medicare premiums until you yourself turn age sixty-five.
4. A. You can reimburse tax-free expenses incurred by your spouse and dependent children, regardless of whether they are covered on your insurance plan or are HSA-eligible themselves.
5. C. Distributions for non-eligible expenses are taxable, regardless of your age. The additional 20% penalty for non-eligible expenses is waived once you turn 65 or are disabled.

6. A. This individual is not your spouse or tax dependent, so you cannot reimburse his or her expenses tax-free (unless your domestic partner is your tax dependent, for example due to disability). Distributions for this individual's expenses are included in your taxable income, and you face an additional 20% tax as a penalty if you are under age sixty-five and not disabled.

7. C. Either one of you can reimburse your own or the other's expenses tax-free from your respective HSAs.

ACCOUNT TRANSFERS OR ROLLOVERS

You can make an unlimited number of trustee-to-trustee transfers from one HSA that you own to another HSA that you own. Under a trustee-to-trustee transfer (the method I strongly recommend for people moving money between HSA accounts), you request that the receiving HSA trustee work directly with the other HSA trustee to complete the transfer. You never take possession of the money. Your custodian will generally have a form that outlines the information needed to complete the transfer. I recommend contacting the bank that you want to transfer from since they will often have stricter requirements than the bank receiving the money. Some trustees will charge a fee for this service. *IRS Notice 2004-50, Q&A 56.*

You can execute one rollover per year. Under a rollover arrangement, you take possession of the funds before depositing them into your new HSA. If you fail to place the funds into a new HSA within sixty days of receipt, your entire rollover is deemed a distribution and included in your taxable income and subject to a 20% additional tax (penalty). You can reduce the impact of the tax on the distribution by applying a portion of eligible expenses not yet reimbursed from the HSA to the distribution. For example, if you fail to redeposit a $2,000 rollover in time but have $800 of unreimbursed expenses, you include only $1,200 in taxable income and pay only an additional $240 additional (20% of $1,200) as a penalty. *IRS Notice 2004-50, Q&A 55.*

You can move balances from an Archer Medical Savings Account (MSA) to an HSA. Archer MSAs, introduced in 1996, are the forerunners of HSAs. You can make an unlimited number of trustee-to-trustee transfers or one rollover annually. While you can keep your funds in an MSA if your trustee continues to offer this program, HSAs are a superior account, and most MSA accountholders are better served moving MSA balances into an HSA (particularly if they are currently participating in an HSA-qualified health plan). *IRS Notice 2004-2, Q&A 23.*

You cannot move unused Health FSA or HRA funds into an HSA. The HOPE Act included provisions for such transfers (though few accountholders actually qualified for the transfer), but the provision expired January 1, 2012. *IRS Notice 2007-22.*

You can make a one-time transfer from a traditional Individual Retirement Arrangement (IRA) or Roth IRA to an HSA. The transfer is subject to the following rules:

- The law limits you to one transfer (or rollover) per lifetime. (Exception: You can make a second transfer in the same year only if your contract type changes from self-only to family coverage.)
- The transferred amount counts against your annual contribution limit in that tax year.
- You must remain HSA-eligible for twelve full months following the month of the transfer. This period is known as the "testing period" (the definition of which differs from the "testing period" associated with making a full contribution during a year that you become HSA-eligible mid-calendar year.)
- If you fail to remain eligible during the testing period, you must include the entire transfer in your taxable income and pay a 20% additional penalty.

- If you have money in two or more IRAs that you wish to transfer to an HSA, you must first do an IRA-to-IRA transfer or rollover to move the money into one transferrable IRA account.

For more information about the IRA-to-HSA transfers, please see Strategy 2 in Section 3, HSA Strategies. *See IRS Notice 2008-51 for detailed information about transfers from an IRA to an HSA.* **You cannot make transfers from any other type of retirement account except a traditional IRA or Roth IRA.** You cannot take advantage of this provision in the law unless your qualified retirement plan is an IRA or is an account type that you can transfer into an IRA before making a transfer into an HSA.

KEY POINTS IN THIS CHAPTER

- You can move funds from one HSA to another, either via one annual rollover (in which you take possession of the funds for a period not to exceed sixty days) or unlimited trustee-to-trustee transfers.
- Trustee to trustee transfers are strongly recommended to avoid mistakes and potential penalties.
- You can transfer funds from an Archer MSA to an HSA.
- You cannot transfer unused balances from a Health FSA or HRA into an HSA.
- You can make a once-per-lifetime transfer from a single traditional IRA or Roth IRA into an HSA, subject to certain restrictions.
- Proceed with caution: The IRA transfer counts against your annual contribution limit, and you must remain HSA-eligible for an additional twelve months after the transfer, which is not always predictable at the time of the transfer.
- See HSA Strategy 4 later in this book to help you determine whether a one-time IRA-to-HSA transfer is right for you.

TEST YOUR KNOWLEDGE

1. **You have a $300 balance remaining in your Health FSA that you want to roll over into your HSA. Which of the following statements is true?**

   A. You can do so if your employer allows it.
   B. You can do so if your FSA administrator and HSA trustee can coordinate the transfer.
   C. You can no longer transfer unused balances from a Health FSA to an HSA.
   D. You must transfer the Health FSA balance to an IRA and then transfer over to your HSA.

2. **You are switching jobs, and your new employer uses a different HSA trustee. Which of the following statements is *not* true?**

   A. You can transfer a portion of or your full balance to the new trustee.
   B. You must spend down your balance in your HSA with your old employer before you can begin to contribute to your new employer's HSA.
   C. You can maintain two HSAs.
   D. You can spend down your balances in your old employer's HSA for eligible expenses without taxes or penalties.

3. **You want to make a one-time transfer from two IRAs to an HSA. Which of the following statements is *not* true?**

   A. If your IRA balance is higher than your annual HSA contribution limit, you'll have to make rollovers in several years to move all your funds.
   B. Your rollover counts against your annual contribution limit.

C. If you lose HSA eligibility during the testing period, the entire amount of the rollover is subject to taxes and a 20% penalty.

D. You must consolidate your IRA balances into a single IRA before you execute the rollover.

TEST YOUR KNOWLEDGE ANSWERS

1. C. The provision allowing a rollover from a Health FSA to an HSA expired January 1, 2012.

2. B. You have the option of retaining balances in your old HSA or moving them to your new trustee. This has no effect on your ability to contribute to your new HSA.

3. A. You are limited to one transfer per lifetime, and the transfer counts against your annual contribution limit. You cannot make transfers over multiple years to increase the total amount that you roll over.

HSA Tax Reporting

You are responsible for HSA tax reporting. You own your HSA, and the reporting requirements are similar to those that you face if you own an IRA. By contrast, a Health FSA and employer-based qualified retirement plan like a 401(k) or 403(b) is a plan owned by the employer. The employer is responsible for standard tax reporting for those programs.

Your employer reports all contributions through a Cafeteria Plan on your W-2 form, issued by January 31 following the tax year. Box 12 of Form W-2 includes all employer contributions and employee pre-tax payroll contributions attributable to the calendar year. This figure is coded with a *W*.

You receive a copy of Form 1099-SA from your HSA trustee by January 31 each year so that you can refer to it as you complete your personal income tax return. This document reports total distributions from the account during the prior tax year. The trustee forwards a copy of Form 1099-SA to the IRS.

Form 1099-SA does not break down distributions for eligible expenses and non-eligible expenses. HSA trustees do not substantiate whether a distribution is for an eligible expense, although some HSA trustees may categorize your transactions based on what you indicated to them when you took the money out. In the end, what matters most is how you categorize your spending to the IRS on Form 8889. You are responsible for tracking eligible and non-eligible distributions.

You receive a copy of Form 5498-SA by May 31 each year. This document reports total contributions to the account during the prior tax year and the fair market value of the HSA. The trustee forwards a copy of this form to the IRS.

Trustees are not required to issue Form 5498-SA until May 31 because you can continue to make contributions for a calendar year up to the earlier of the date that you file your income tax returns or the due date for federal tax returns (generally April 15). Thus, you must rely on other documentation—such as W-2s, account statements, and web-based transaction searches—to report your HSA contributions on your income tax returns. Some HSA trustees now send a 5498-SA in January based on your calendar year activity and then send a revised form in May just to those accountholders who make prior-year deposits.

You complete and submit Form 8889 as part of your federal income tax return. Form 8889 captures your contributions (except for employer contributions and your pre-tax payroll contributions through your employer's Cafeteria Plan) and your distributions. You indicate the total value of distributions for both eligible and non-eligible expenses. You calculate any additions to taxable income, penalties for distributions for non-eligible expenses and testing period violations.

TEST YOUR KNOWLEDGE

1. **You are preparing to file your tax return. Which of the following statements is *not* true?**

   A. You must file Form 8889 with your tax return.

   B. You do not have to submit receipts with your tax return.

   C. You indicate total distributions and include the sum of distributions for eligible and non-eligible expenses.

   D. You have Form 1099-SA and Form 5498-SA by
      January 31 to assist in your tax return preparation.

**2. Which of the following statements is true of Form
   1099-SA?**

   A. Your trustee issues copies to you and the IRS.
   B. It includes all contributions and distributions
      from your HSA.
   C. Your trustee is required to issue it by May 31.
   D. It breaks down distributions for eligible and non-
      eligible expenses.

**3. Which of the following statements about Form 5498-
   SA is *not* true?**

   A. You receive a preliminary copy by January 31.
   B. It shows all contributions attributable to that
      calendar year.
   C. It shows the fair market value of your HSA.
   D. Your trustee sends copies to you and the IRS.

TEST YOUR KNOWLEDGE ANSWERS

1. D. Your trustee is not required to issue Form 5498-SA
   until May 31 since you can make contributions for a
   calendar year up to the time that you file your tax return
   for that year (generally April 15).
2. A. Form 1099-SA includes distribution information only,
   your trustee must issue it by January 31, and it shows total
   distributions without a breakdown of eligible and non-
   eligible expenses (which a typical trustee does not track).
3. A. Trustees are not required to issue Form 5498-SA until
   May 31, as explained above.

YOUR HSA TRUSTEE

HSAs are offered by trustees or custodians. While there are legal differences in the fiduciary responsibilities of trustees and custodians, they perform the same duties in managing HSAs. This book refers to trustees and custodians collectively as "trustees."

Your HSA trust agreement cannot limit your reimbursements to eligible expenses. Neither your trustee nor your employer can require that you reimburse only eligible expenses. The IRS law gives you the freedom to make distributions for any expense (subject to income taxes and penalties if the expenses are not HSA-eligible), and no one can restrict your freedom. *IRS Notice 2004-50, Q&A 79.*

Your trustee must provide at least one way for you to make distributions for non-eligible expenses. Since you are entitled to make distributions for non-eligible expenses, your trustee must provide you with a convenient means for doing so. A trustee typically will offer an unrestricted debit card (accepted at all merchant locations) and at least one other method of distributions. Options include checkbook access, a process to request that the trustee write a check to you and online bill pay through the HSA website.

Your trustee can place certain restrictions on distributions. HSA trustees are allowed to place "reasonable" restrictions on the amount and timing of your HSA distributions. They can, for example, not allow cash withdrawals with your HSA debit card, not allow a reimbursement under $10 or limit the number of checks that you write or debit card transactions that you complete in a given month. Some trustees will restrict the types of merchants at which your debit card can be used or even issue a card that only works for items in the store that are IRS approved for medical reimbursement. These terms are spelled out in your agreement with the HSA trustee. If you do not like the terms, you can change trustees at any time. *IRS Notice 2004-50, Q&A 80.*

Your HSA trustee does not track which distributions are for eligible expenses. You own your HSA. You are responsible for account compliance, including knowing which distributions are for eligible expenses and reporting your activity annually on your income tax return.

Your HSA trustee does not track your deposits to ensure that you do not exceed your maximum annual contribution. A trustee typically sets an annual contribution limit equal to the statutory maximum annual contribution for a family contract ($6,750 in 2016), plus an additional $1,000 (representing the catch-up contribution) if you represent your age as fifty-five or older. Your trustee, however, usually has no way of knowing whether you are covered by a self-only contract or whether you are eligible during all twelve months of the calendar year. Thus, the trustee cannot set its system to limit your contributions to your actual contribution limit, although some trustees are introducing self-service tools that will help you calculate and keep track of your own limits. You are responsible for knowing the rules and limiting your contributions to the maximum that applies to you in your situation.

Your trustee does not have to accept a rollover or trustee-to-trustee transfer from another HSA or an Archer MSA. Trustees typically have processes in place to accept such inflows of assets, though the law does not require them to do so. Trustees have well-established processes for accepting IRA rollovers and transfers, and most have modified these processes to accommodate HSAs.

Your trustee must surrender balances if you want to move funds from that trustee via a rollover or trustee-to-trustee transfer. While trustees can choose whether or not to *accept* transfers or rollovers, they do not have an option not to *surrender* any portion of or your entire balance if you want to withdraw funds for any reason. Trustees typically charge an account closure fee (generally $20 or $25), especially when you are asking them to do work to transfer your money to another trustee. You may be able to avoid this fee by writing a check on your old account for the balance and depositing that check within sixty days into your new HSA as a "rollover" transaction. In this case, be sure to complete your new trustee's rollover paperwork to ensure that the deposit is reflected as a rollover rather than a new contribution since you have already received a tax benefit for that deposit when it was originally made.

TEST YOUR KNOWLEDGE

1. **Your employer makes a substantial employer contribution to your HSA and wants to make sure you use the funds only for eligible expenses. Which of the following statements below is true?**

    A. Your employer works with the trustee to insert a clause in your HSA trust agreement.

    B. Your employer must petition the IRS to enforce this restriction.

    C. Your employer cannot impose this restriction.

    D. You are responsible for documenting to your employer that you have distributions for eligible expenses at least equal to your employer contribution.

2. **You want to roll over funds from an HSA that you set up with a former employer. Which of the following statements below is true?**
   A. Your new trustee must accept these rollover funds.
   B. Your former trustee must surrender the funds.
   C. You are not allowed to make the rollover. You must spend down your balance in your former HSA.
   D. The rollover happens automatically.

3. **Which of the services below does an HSA trustee typically *not* provide?**
   A. Acceptance of trustee-to-trustee transfer.
   B. Acceptance of rollover funds.
   C. An ironclad system to ensure that you do not exceed your statutory maximum annual contribution based on your unique situation.
   D. At least one means of making distributions for non-eligible expenses.

TEST YOUR KNOWLEDGE ANSWERS

1. C. Your employer cannot impose such restrictions, and an HSA trust agreement cannot contain such language.
2. B. You are allowed to make rollovers at any time. Rollovers never happen automatically because an HSA is an individual account not tied to an employer and trustees are not required to accept rollovers (but they typically do).
3. C. A trustee does not know or track any activity that might impact your maximum contribution, including such factors as a spouse's Health FSA, your accessing ineligible care through the VA or your enrolling in Medicare midyear.

PART 2
HSAs and Situations

SITUATION NUMBER 1

HSAS AND MEDICARE

Medicare and its impact on HSAs is one of the least understood aspects of the Health Savings Account program. In fact, Medicare itself is often confusing for individuals, so let's start by defining Medicare. Medicare is a federal government program that provides health coverage to individuals who are age sixty-five or older or disabled (as defined by Section 179 of the IRC).

For a much more comprehensive discussion of Medicare, you can refer to *Medicare and You*, an annual guide published by the Centers for Medicare and Medicaid Services (CMS), an agency of the US Department of Health and Human Services. You can locate an electronic version of *Medicare and You* through a search engine.

Standard Medicare coverage is composed of three parts:

Part A: A cornerstone of the original Medicare legislation passed in 1965, Part A covers hospitalization, skilled nursing stays, home health, and hospice. Employees and their employers pay payroll taxes during employees' working years (current tax rate: 2.9% of taxable income, divided evenly between employee and employer). Individuals who have paid into the system for forty calendar quarters (ten years) receive Part A at no cost. Others can purchase Part A for a monthly premium up to $407 (2015 figure). Individuals do not have to enroll in Part A when they are first eligible. If they do not enroll immediately and their coverage is subject to premium, they may face a penalty of up to 10% additional premium for double the number of years that they delayed enrollment.

Part B: The second element of the original Medicare legislation, Part B covers a broad range of outpatient services, including physician visits, chiropractic care, lab work, outpatient therapy, behavioral health, and prosthetics, as well as select preventive services. It also covers emergency and urgent care services. All enrollees pay a monthly premium, which is deducted from Social Security checks when the individual is receiving Social Security benefits. The monthly premium in 2015 is $104.90 for most enrollees, although those with higher retirement incomes two years prior (2013 income for 2015 premiums) may face monthly premiums as high as $335.70. Individuals must enroll in Part B when they are first eligible, or after that date immediately after they lose other coverage that CMS deems "creditable coverage." Failure to enroll during these time periods results in a penalty in the form of additional premium.

Part A and Part B are often referred to as "Original Medicare" because they were the only two parts of the program included in the original 1965 law.

Part D: Part D, which covers prescription drugs, came into law through the Medicare Prescription Drug, Improvement, and Modernization Act of 2003, which is the same legislation that created HSAs. Like Part B, Part D carries a premium, as well as penalties in the form of additional premium for members who do not enroll when first eligible or immediately after losing "creditable coverage." Unlike original Medicare (Parts A and B), Medicare Part D benefits are delivered by private insurers. Individuals enrolled in Part A and Part B and eligible to enroll in Part D choose a prescription drug program administered by a private insurer.

Part D premiums vary by plan, so eligible individuals can choose the plan that provides the right coverage at the right price to meet their particular needs. In addition to premiums that the private plan charges, members face additional premiums of $12.30 to $70.80 if their 2013 income exceeded $85,000.

So you ask, what about Part C? There is a Part C, but it is completely different from the other parts. Individuals who are eligible to enroll in Part A and Part B have the option to enroll in a Medicare Advantage (Part C) plan offered by a private insurer. In this arrangement, CMS pays the private insurer a monthly stipend (which varies by geographic area) to provide coverage in place of Medicare. The private insurer may provide additional services, may offer a limited network, and can charge a premium in addition to the money that it receives from CMS. The private insurer assumes the risk, such that if the cost of treating that individual exceeds the CMS payment (and member premium, if applicable), the private insurer (not CMS) is financially responsible for those additional costs.

ENROLLING IN MEDICARE

Individuals are often confused about how and when they are enrolled in Medicare. The common perception is that individuals are enrolled automatically in Part A when they reach age 65. This is not the case, however. Rather, individuals become enrolled in Part A in one of two ways:

- They apply and are approved to receive Social Security benefits, which triggers their automatic enrollment in Social Security (unless they receive Social Security benefits before age sixty-five, in which case their automatic enrollment in Medicare is delayed until they reach age sixty-five).
- They apply for Part A benefits at age sixty-five, or earlier, if they meet the IRC definition of disabled or are suffering from End-Stage Renal Disease (ESRD) or amyotrophic lateral sclerosis (ALS, or Lou Gehrig's disease).

Key takeaway: An individual who does not want to enroll in Part A can delay enrollment by not signing up to receive Social Security benefits and not applying for Part A benefits. Traditionally, individuals enrolled in Part A automatically, even if they remained actively at work (or a spouse remained actively at work) and were covered on their employers' group coverage. Since most individuals receive Part A premium-free, they experienced no downside to receiving this coverage, even if benefits were secondary to an employer's plan and thus did not provide any additional level of coverage. In the HSA world, Part A-eligible individuals must weigh carefully their decision whether or not to enroll in Part A because it has implications for HSA eligibility.

Medicare Part B and Part D are available only to those who affirmatively apply for benefits. An individual chooses whether to enroll in Part B and/or Part D, making that choice upon turning age sixty-five, immediately after losing Medicare creditable coverage (coverage deemed at least as rich as Medicare, as determined by CMS) after age sixty-five or during Medicare's annual open enrollment period after age sixty-five. Individuals who enroll after age sixty-five and do not have Medicare creditable coverage prior to enrolling in Part B and/or Part D may be subject to Part B and Part D premium penalties. See *Medicare and You*, 2014 edition (available online), Section 2 (Part B), and Section 6 (Part D) for more details.

So with this background, let's explore all aspects of Medicare that are relevant to individuals who are or want to become HSA-eligible.

ELIGIBILITY

If you are enrolled in any Part of Medicare, you are no longer HSA-eligible since Medicare plan designs do not meet the criteria for a qualified plan. If you are not yet enrolled in Medicare, you must delay enrollment in Medicare when you are initially eligible if you want to continue contributing to your

HSA. If you are already enrolled in any Part of Medicare, you cannot be HSA-eligible.

In this situation, it is important to remember that an individual does not have to be the health plan subscriber to be HSA-eligible. If you enroll in Part A, continue to work and continue to cover yourself and your spouse on your employer's HSA-qualified plan, your spouse may be HSA-eligible. In that case, he or she can open an HSA, either or both of you can contribute to his or her HSA and he or she can reimburse eligible expenses that each of you incurs. *IRC Section 223((b)(7)* and *IRS Notice 2004-50, Q&A 2.*

You do not lose your HSA eligibility if a family member is enrolled in Medicare. All Medicare policies are individual contracts. A family member's enrollment in Medicare does not impact your HSA eligibility, as long as you yourself are not enrolled in Medicare. *IRS Notice 2008-59, Q&A 11*

Once you are enrolled in Medicare, you effectively lose your HSA eligibility forever. If you are enrolled in Part A and remain covered on your employer's health plan, and your employer offers a new HSA-qualified health plan, you can enroll in that health plan. In practical terms, though, you cannot become HSA-eligible. To do so, you have to disenroll from Medicare. And you cannot disenroll from Medicare without disenrolling from Social Security, if you are receiving Social Security benefits. To disenroll from either program, you must pay back all benefits received through that specific program.

A federal district court confirmed this policy in early 2012 in the case of Hall v. Sebelius. Three plaintiffs, including former US House Majority Leader Dick Armey (R-Tex.), filed suit because they wanted to collect Social Security without enrolling in Medicare (which did not provide as rich coverage as their retiree coverage). Thus, their attempt to decouple Social Security enrollment from Medicare enrollment was not HSA-related. The federal district court ruled against them and reaffirmed the link between Social Security and Medicare.

Now, if you are age sixty-seven, are healthy, and have enrolled in premium-free Part A only and not another Part of Medicare or Social Security, repaying scant Medicare Part A benefits might not have much of an economic impact on you. On the other hand, if you are age sixty-nine and have had some health issues and have collected Social Security benefits since age sixty-five, you may have to pay back a huge sum of money to reimburse Social Security and Medicare benefits to disenroll. Under this latter scenario, it is inconceivable that an individual who enrolls in an HSA program can ever gain tax advantages sufficient to overcome the costs associated with disenrollment from Social Security and Part A.

If you are enrolled in Medicare and thus are not HSA-eligible, and you cover yourself and your spouse on your employer's HSA-qualified health plan, your spouse may be HSA-eligible. Yes, there may be a way to receive the benefits associated with an HSA, even if you are no longer HSA-eligible. The concept is simple: Individuals do not have to be health plan subscribers to be HSA-eligible. Thus, if your employer offers an HSA-qualified plan that covers you and your spouse, and you are enrolled in Medicare, your spouse might meet the general eligibility criteria to open and contribute to an HSA. *IRC Section 223((b)(7)* and *IRS Notice 2004-50, Q&A 2.*

CONTRIBUTIONS

You can continue to contribute to an HSA after your sixty-fifth birthday, as long as you remain HSA-eligible. A sixty-fifth birthday is a milestone but by itself does not impact an individual's HSA eligibility. As long as you are HSA-eligible and do not enroll in any Part of Medicare, you can still contribute to an HSA. Once you enroll in any Part of Medicare at age sixty-five or older (or younger, if you are disabled or diagnosed with end-stage renal disease or Lou Gehrig's disease), you lose your HSA eligibility. *IRS Notice 2004-50, Q&A 2.*

If you are enrolled on a family contract on your employer's group insurance and you are no longer HSA-eligible, you might still be able to reduce your taxable income through an HSA. Individuals do not have to be health plan subscribers to be HSA-eligible. An individual subscriber's spouse may be HSA-eligible, in which case the spouse can fund his or her own HSA.

Your employer can contribute to your spouse's HSA. If you are not HSA-eligible but your spouse is, your employer might choose to give your spouse the same employer contribution that it offers to other employees. In another case, your employer might encourage you to receive coverage through your spouse's employer's HSA-qualified plan by offering to contribute to your spouse's HSA. In either situation, your employer can make a contribution to your spouse's plan. The contribution is included in your taxable income, and your spouse can deduct it on his or her personal income tax return (or the two of you can deduct it on your joint tax return). Employers need to be careful that they do not engage in discriminatory practices by selectively offering this benefit to certain employees only. *IRS Notice 2008-59, Q&A 26.*

If you cover at least one additional family member, you are subject to family contribution limits, even if only one person on the contract is HSA-eligible. It is not uncommon for a family to retain group coverage while one spouse remains actively working and either spouse is enrolled in Medicare. In this case, as long as one of you is HSA-eligible, that individual can contribute up to the statutory maximum annual contribution for a family contract (plus an additional $1,000 annually if age 55 or older)— amounts that are pro-rated if the individual is not HSA-eligible all twelve months.

In this case, a spouse can fund his or her own HSA and make contributions up to the family limit. *IRS Notice 2008-59, Q&A 16.*

DISTRIBUTIONS

Once you are enrolled in Medicare and are no longer HSA-eligible, you can continue to make tax-free distributions for eligible expenses. This rule holds true for all accountholders, regardless of whether they are no longer HSA-eligible due to enrollment in Medicare or any other disqualifying event. You never lose the ability to make tax-free distributions. *IRS Notice 2004-2, Q&A 25.*

If your spouse is enrolled in Medicare, you can still reimburse his or her eligible expenses (subject to one limitation in the next paragraph) tax-free from your HSA. You can reimburse any eligible individual's (your own, your spouse's, and your tax dependents') eligible expenses tax-free, whether not that individual is HSA-eligible or is or ever was (a) enrolled on your health plan or (b) HSA-eligible. *IRS Notice 2004-50, Q&A 36.*

You cannot reimburse your own or any individual's Medicare or qualifying retiree policy premiums tax-free from your HSA until you, the accountholder, turn age sixty-five. Not many people understand this provision. You cannot make tax-free distributions to reimburse anyone's (your own, your spouse's or a disabled tax dependent's) Medicare premiums until you turn age sixty-five. If your family has only one HSA owner and that accountholder is the older spouse, this issue does not surface as long as you do not begin to pay Medicare premiums before age sixty-five.

By contrast, planning becomes more important if the younger spouse is the family's sole HSA owner. In this case, if the older spouse is HSA-eligible prior to turning age sixty-five, have the older spouse open an HSA and contribute enough to his or her HSA to cover his or her Medicare premiums at least until the primary accountholder turns age sixty-five. This strategy may involve splitting the annual family contribution between the two HSAs, or the older spouse may place the entire family contribution into his or her HSA. Both spouses, if eligible, can make contributions to their own HSAs. *IRC Section 223(d)(2)(C)(iv)* and *IRS Notice 2004-50, Q&A 44.*

TEST YOUR KNOWLEDGE

1. **Your spouse is age sixty-seven, and you are age sixty-four. Your spouse asks you to reimburse her Medicare premiums from your HSA. Can you make tax-free distributions from your HSA to reimburse her Medicare premiums?**

    A. Yes. As long as she is your spouse, you can reimburse her Medicare premiums tax-free from your HSA.

    B. Yes, you can reimburse her Part B premium tax-free because it is part of Original Medicare, but Part D premiums are not eligible for tax-free reimbursement from an HSA.

    C. No. While Medicare premiums are an eligible expense, you cannot make tax-free distributions from your HSA because you yourself have not reached age sixty-five.

    D. No. Medicare premiums are not an eligible expense, and you cannot make any distributions from your HSA for ineligible expenses.

2. **You are HSA-eligible and turning age sixty-five next month. Which of the following statements is true?**

    A. You must enroll in Medicare Part A, but you can delay enrollment in Parts B and D and remain HSA-eligible.

    B. You can remain HSA-eligible as long as you do not enroll in Medicare.

    C. You must enroll in Medicare Part C but can delay enrollment in Original Medicare (Part A and Part B) and thereby remain HSA-eligible.

    D. You lose HSA eligibility at age sixty-five, whether or not you enroll in Medicare.

3. **You (age fifty-six) and your spouse (age sixty-nine) are enrolled on your HSA plan. He's also enrolled in Medicare Part A. How much can you contribute to your HSA?**

   A. The statutory maximum for a family contract, plus a catch-up contribution for you.
   B. The statutory maximum for a self-only contract, plus your catch-up contribution.
   C. The statutory maximum for a family contract, plus a catch-up contribution for each of you.
   D. You cannot contribute to an HSA because your spouse is enrolled in Medicare.

4. **You (age sixty-six) and your spouse (age seventy) always maintained separate individual health insurance contracts. He never enrolled in an HSA-qualified plan. He's enrolled in Medicare. Which of the following statements is true?**

   A. You cannot reimburse his HSA-eligible expenses from your HSA because he was never covered on your insurance.
   B. You can reimburse his expenses from your HSA, but those distributions are subject to income tax and a 30% penalty.
   C. You cannot reimburse his expenses from your HSA, but he can create his own HSA, you can transfer a portion of your balance to his HSA, and he can reimburse his expenses tax-free from his HSA.
   D. You can reimburse his expenses tax-free because he's your spouse, regardless of his past or present coverage.

5. **You and your spouse are covered on your HSA-qualified plan and are both HSA-eligible. You are**

the accountholder for the HSA containing all family contributions. You are age forty-eight, and your spouse just celebrated his fifty-fifth birthday. Which of the following statements is true?

 A. Your spouse can make a catch-up contribution, but he must open his own HSA into which he can make the contribution.

 B. Your spouse cannot make a catch-up contribution because he is not the health plan subscriber.

 C. Your spouse cannot make a catch-up contribution until you, the family accountholder, turn age sixty-five.

 D. Your spouse can make a catch-up contribution, but it is not tax-deductible because he's not the health plan subscriber.

Test Your Knowledge Answers

1. C. While you can reimburse your spouse's other eligible expenses tax-free, you cannot reimburse your spouse's or your own Medicare premiums tax-free until you, the accountholder, turn age sixty-five. Of course, you can always make distributions for any expenses, including Medicare premiums before you turn age sixty-five, but such distributions are included in your taxable income and subject to a 20% additional tax (penalty).

2. B. You do not have to enroll in any Part of Medicare upon turning age sixty-five and becoming eligible to enroll. And unless you are age sixty-five or older and enroll in Social Security, you will not be enrolled in any Part of Medicare unless you apply for benefits.

3. A. As long as you are enrolled on a family contract, regardless of whether anyone else enrolled on the contract is HSA-eligible, you can make a family contribution.

And since you are age fifty-five or older, you can make an additional $1,000 catch-up contribution.

4. D. Remember, when it comes to distributions, coverage does not matter. The only relevant factor is an individual's relationship to you. He's your spouse. You can reimburse a spouse's eligible expenses tax-free.

5. A. An individual does not have to be the health plan subscriber to be HSA-eligible. In this case, the husband is HSA-eligible and age fifty-five. Therefore, he can make a catch-up contribution. Under current law, an individual's catch-up contribution must go into his or her own HSA.

SITUATION NUMBER 2

HSAS AND HEALTH FSAS

Next to Medicare, the most confusing aspects of an HSA's relationship to another product or program revolve around Health FSAs. A Health FSA, as described in chapter 3, is an employer-sponsored program that allows employees to elect to receive a portion of their compensation in the form of pre-tax contributions to an account out of which they can draw funds tax-free to pay for certain health-related expenses. This brief description sounds a lot like an HSA, though Health FSAs and HSAs differ in many respects:

Health FSA: Participant forfeits unused funds back to the employer (though an October 2013 change permits an employer to allow participating employees to roll over up to $500 per year).

HSA: Unused funds are available year after year without limit for future use.

Health FSA: Participant is locked into an annual election.

HSA: Accountholders can vary their contributions throughout the year and even until tax day following each tax year.

Health FSA: All contributions are through pre-tax payroll.

HSA: Accountholders can make pre-tax payroll or personal contributions.

Health FSA: Balances do not earn interest and cannot be invested.

HSA: Balances earn interest and can be invested.

Health FSA: Participation is limited to employees whose employer offers the program.

HSA: Anyone who meets eligibility requirements can participate.

Health FSA: Participants must substantiate expenses at time of purchase.

HSA: Substantiation is required only if a participant's personal income tax return is audited.

Health FSA: Participants are not required to make additional tax filings.

HSA: Accountholders must complete a form on personal tax return.

Health FSA: Participants can spend the entire annual election at any time.

HSA: Accountholders can spend no more than the current account balance.

ELIGIBILITY

You are not HSA-eligible if you participate in your employer's general Health FSA, which reimburses all Section 213(d) expenses. The IRS considers a Health FSA a health plan. A general Health FSA does not meet the requirements of an HSA-qualified plan (its design does not include a minimum deductible before it begins to pay benefits). Therefore, anyone who is eligible to receive benefits through a general Health FSA is not HSA-eligible. *IRS Rev. Rul. 2004-45, Situation 1.*

You (and your spouse) are not HSA-eligible if your spouse is enrolled in a general Health FSA through his or her employer (and your spouse is not HSA-eligible, either). Under federal tax law, a Health FSA subscriber, his or her spouse (federal definition) and his or her tax dependents all are eligible to receive reimbursement through a Health FSA. Therefore, these individuals can have health coverage that is not permitted under HSA eligibility rules. This holds true whether or not the individuals actually seek reimbursement for any eligible expenses.

Your opportunity to enroll in an HSA-qualified plan during your general Health FSA year is not a qualifying event that allows you to eliminate your participation in the Health FSA. While there are certain qualifying life events (including marriage, divorce, birth, adoption, and death) under which you can change your participation or election in a Health FSA, seeking immediate HSA eligibility is not one of them. You are locked into your Health FSA for the balance of the Health FSA plan year, even if you exhaust your entire election before the end of the plan year.

You or your federally recognized spouse can enroll in a Limited-Purpose Health FSA without impacting your HSA eligibility. A Limited-Purpose Health FSA reimburses dental, vision, and preventive care expenses only. The HSA eligibility rules specifically allow individuals to have dental and vision coverage without impacting their HSA eligibility. The law further allows for first-dollar coverage for preventive care under an HSA-qualified plan. Therefore, a Health FSA that limits reimbursement to this subset of Section 213(d) expenses does not compromise HSA eligibility. Note, though, that the plan document must specifically limit reimbursement, and the administrator must administer the plan properly. An individual who can receive reimbursement through a general Health FSA cannot become HSA-eligible by merely not seeking reimbursement for any expenses other than dental, vision, and preventive care. *IRC Section (c)(1)(B)(I), Section (c)(2)(C)* and *IRS Rev. Rul. 2004-45, Situation 2.*

You or your federally recognized spouse can enroll in a Post-Deductible Health FSA without impacting your HSA eligibility. A Post-Deductible Health FSA does not begin to pay benefits until you've incurred eligible expenses no less than the statutory minimum annual deductible for an HSA-qualified plan ($1,300 for a self-only and $2,600 for a family contract in

2016). In this case, the Health FSA becomes an HSA-qualified plan, and you are now enrolled in two HSA-qualified plans. Post-Deductible Health FSAs are not common because they require a degree of coordination between the health plan and the Health FSA administrator, or must rely on the word of the subscriber, to determine when the minimum deductible is met. *IRS Rev. Rul. 2004-45, Situation 4.*

Some administrators offer a hybrid Limited-Purpose and Post-Deductible Health FSA. You may enroll in a limited Health FSA that combines the best of both designs. The Health FSA is designed like a Limited-Purpose Health FSA, with reimbursement for only dental, vision, and preventive services. Once you certify to the administrator that you have met the statutory minimum annual deductible for your contract type ($1,300 for self-only and $2,600 for family coverage in 2016), you can spend the balance of your election on any FSA-qualified expense—just as you can with a Post-Deductible Health FSA.

OVERLAPPING COVERAGE: HEALTH FSA AND HSA-QUALIFIED PLAN

You cannot end your participation in a general Health FSA before the end of the plan year to gain HSA eligibility. You may be in the middle of a general Health FSA plan year—your own or your spouse's—when your employer (or your spouse's) offers an HSA-qualified plan on your health plan anniversary date. You cannot opt out of your general Health FSA early, nor can you zero out your balance prior to the effective date of your HSA-qualified health plan, to gain immediate HSA eligibility. You remain enrolled in your Health FSA through the entire plan year, regardless of remaining balance. You can enroll in an HSA-qualified health plan while you are covered under a general Health FSA (even with no balance remaining), but you cannot open and contribute to an HSA until you no longer have conflicting coverage.

Your employer can alter your Health FSA plan, if its plan documents allow, to allow you and other health insurance subscribers in the company to become HSA-eligible immediately. Your employer may be able to modify the Health FSA program midyear, either by (1) eliminating it entirely the day before the HSA-qualified health plan becomes effective or (2) changing the Health FSA to a Limited-Purpose Health FSA beginning with the effective date of the HSA-qualified health plan. In either situation, the plan change, if allowed by the employer's plan documents, impacts all Health FSA participants, including those who do not seek HSA eligibility. The first option increases participant forfeitures since enrollees cannot alter their elections once the employer changes the terms of the Health FSA. With the second option, the risk of forfeiture is reduced since participants can still spend balances on dental, vision, and preventive care. However, participants still face the prospect of having overfunded their Health FSAs based on the original broader range of expenses that were eligible for reimbursement.

If your general Health FSA has a grace period (an additional 2½ months during which you can continue to accumulate expenses eligible for reimbursement), you can become HSA-eligible prior to the beginning of the grace period. A provision in the law accommodates individuals whose employers have adopted the grace period. If you are in this situation, you can spend down your Health FSA cash balance to zero by the end of the twelve-month year (prior to the first day of the grace period). Your account must show a zero balance on your administrator's books. It is not enough to have unsubmitted receipts that will zero out your balance by the end of the twelve-month plan year; you must actually submit those expenses and have no balance reflected before the end of the twelve-month plan year. If you miss this opportunity by having a remaining balance (of even a minuscule amount) in your Health FSA at the beginning of the grace period, you cannot become HSA-eligible before the first day of the first month after the end of the grace period.

Your employer can offer HSA eligibility remedies for its entire Health FSA population covered by a grace period. Your employer can take action to make all employees HSA-eligible at the beginning of the Health FSA grace period, if its plan documents allow, by acting before the end of the twelve-month plan year to either (1) eliminate the grace period or (2) change the grace period to a Limited-Purpose Health FSA. As discussed above, this Health FSA plan change impacts all participants, not just those who seek HSA eligibility, and may increase participant forfeitures of unused balances. *IRS Notice 2005-86, Situation 2.*

If your Health FSA includes a rollover of up to $500, you need to act to protect your HSA eligibility. In October 2013, the IRS ruled that employers could amend their Health FSA plans to allow a rollover of up to $500 into the following plan year. Under this provision, participants can roll over a limited balance amount for an unlimited time period. (By contrast, the grace period allows an unlimited balance amount rollover for a limited time.) The IRS says there are three ways to act to preserve your HSA eligibility when transitioning from a Health FSA with a rollover feature. First, as with the grace period, if the Health FSA participant spends her entire FSA balance by the end of the Health FSA plan year, she can become HSA-eligible as soon as she enrolls in the HSA-qualified plan (assuming that she is otherwise HSA-eligible). Second, employers may allow employees choose before the end of the plan year to transfer funds into a Limited-Purpose FSA. Employers are also allowed to automatically move employees' unused dollars into a Limited-Purpose FSA for all who select an HSA-qualified plan in the following plan year. Finally, the IRS allows for employers to give the option for an employee to simply decline or waive participation in the balance rollover provision to maintain HSA eligibility. (IRS Memorandum 201413005 dated 3/28/14).

You do not lose HSA eligibility because you enroll in a dependent care Flexible Spending Arrangement. A Dependent Care Reimbursement Account (DCRA) reimburses child-care (nursery, pre-school, after-school, and summer day camp expenses for children under age thirteen) expenses and certain expenses for watching disabled children age thirteen and older and dependent adults while you (and your spouse, if you are married) work or go to school. Your participation in a DCRA program does not impact your HSA eligibility because the program does not reimburse medical expenses.

CONTRIBUTIONS

You can contribute to a Limited-Purpose or Post-Deductible Health FSA without impacting your HSA contribution. Your employer determines your maximum election into your Limited-Purpose or Post-Deductible Health FSA, consistent with IRS regulations (which limit elections to all Health FSAs to no more than $2,550, effective January 1, 2015, and indexed annually thereafter). Your Health FSA election is independent of your HSA contribution and does not reduce the maximum contribution that you can make to your Health FSA.

DISTRIBUTIONS

You can choose to reimburse an eligible dental, vision, or preventive care expense from your Limited-Purpose Health FSA or HSA. You decide from which account to reimburse these eligible expenses. The IRS imposes no payment ordering rules. Generally, you'll want to spend money from your Health FSA first if the expense can be reimbursed from the Health FSA since you forfeit any unused balances at the end of the year.

If you remain enrolled in a general Health FSA during the beginning of the period that you are covered under an HSA-qualified plan, you can use your Health FSA election to reimburse all eligible expenses. If you are not HSA-eligible when you first enroll in an HSA-qualified plan and have a Health FSA in force, you can use your Health FSA funds to reimburse all Section 213(d) expenses (subject to any limits that your employer imposes on the range of eligible expenses, which usually is minimal if any). Unfortunately, you cannot change your election midyear, even if your new health plan increases your out-of-pocket responsibility. *IRC Section 223(c)(1)(B)(iii) as amended* and *Health Opportunity Patient Empowerment Act of 2006, Section 5(b)*.

KEY POINTS IN THIS CHAPTER

- A general Health FSA is not permitted coverage for HSA accountholders. You cannot be covered on a general Health FSA and become or remain HSA-eligible.
- You are enrolled in a Health FSA if your spouse participates in his or her employer's Health FSA.
- You cannot disenroll midyear from a Health FSA to gain HSA eligibility.
- Your employer may be able to alter the terms of its general Health FSA to allow employees to gain HSA eligibility when they first enroll in an HSA-qualified plan. The Health FSA plan changes apply to all employees and may result in increased forfeitures.
- You can, and your employer may be able to, take action so that you can become HSA-eligible immediately prior to the beginning of a Health FSA grace period.
- You can make an election to a Limited-Purpose Health FSA without impacting your maximum contribution to your HSA.
- When an expense is eligible for distribution from both a Limited-Purpose Health FSA and an HSA, you determine from which account you make the distribution.

Consumer Checklist

✓ Make sure you understand your spouse's benefit elections through her employer so that her actions do not impact your HSA eligibility.

✓ Educate your spouse about the impact of his future benefit decision to make sure he does not create a conflict in the future.

✓ Understand the implications if you participate in your employer's general Health FSA that does not run concurrent with the health insurance, and your employer introduces an HSA-qualified health plan.

✓ Be sure to understand the implications of a grace or rollover period and what action you can take to become HSA-eligible before the first day of a grace or rollover period.

Test Your Knowledge

1. **You are enrolled in a general Health FSA that continues through the first months of your HSA-qualified health plan. Which of the following statements is true?**

   A. You are not HSA-eligible until the end of the Health FSA plan year, but you can pay for eligible expenses tax-free from your Health FSA election.

   B. You can terminate your participation in the Health FSA. Enrolling in an HSA program is a qualifying event to terminate Health FSA coverage.

   C. You can become HSA-eligible immediately as long as you have no balance remaining in your Health FSA as of the first day of your coverage under the HSA-qualified plan.

   D. You are not HSA-eligible until the end of the Health FSA plan year, but you can make a one-time increase in your Health FSA election to cover your increased expenses under the HSA-qualified health plan.

2. **Your long-time domestic partner participates in his employer's general Health FSA. What are the implications for your HSA eligibility?**

   A. You cannot become HSA-eligible before the end of his Health FSA plan year.

   B. You can become HSA-eligible if you submit a letter to his employer's Health FSA administrator promising not to seek future reimbursement.

   C. It has no impact on you because you are not eligible to receive reimbursements from his Health FSA.

   D. You cannot become HSA-eligible before the end of his Health FSA plan year, but you can reimburse eligible expenses from his Health FSA.

3. **You have both an HSA and a Limited-Purpose Health FSA. You have a $700 bill for a root canal. Which of the following reimbursement options is true?**

   A. You must use Health FSA funds first, then HSA balances.

   B. Your employer determines from which account you can reimburse the expense.

   C. Dental expenses are not eligible for reimbursement from a Limited-Purpose Health FSA. You must use your HSA or personal funds.

   D. You choose from which account to reimburse the expense.

4. **Your employer wants to alter the terms of its general Health FSA with a 2½-month grace period so that you and your co-workers can become HSA-eligible immediately. Which of the following actions is *not* an option for your employer?**

   A. Terminate the grace period completely if plan documents allow.

     B. Turn the grace period into a Limited-Purpose Health if plan documents allow.

     C. Instruct employees to spend and receive reimbursement for their entire Health FSA elections prior to the beginning of the grace period.

     D. Permit employees who want to be HSA-eligible to opt out of the Health FSA prior to the beginning of the grace period.

TEST YOUR KNOWLEDGE ANSWERS

1. A. You cannot terminate participation in a Health FSA without a qualifying event, you cannot change your election to reimburse higher expenses and you remain covered by a Health FSA through the end of the plan year, even if you no longer have a balance.

2. C. Since you are not married to your domestic partner, you cannot receive reimbursement from his Health FSA, whether or not you are HSA-eligible.

3. D. Your employer, Health FSA administrator or HSA trustee does not set payment order rules. When an expense can be reimbursed from a Limited-Purpose Health FSA or HSA, you, the accountholder, decide. In most cases, if makes sense to use the Limited Purpose FSA first because the funds are time-limited.

4. D. Health FSA participants cannot opt out of the program without a qualifying event. Seeking to gain HSA eligibility is not a qualifying event.

SITUATION NUMBER 3

HSAS AND CERTAIN BUSINESS OWNERS

Federal tax law places restrictions on certain business owners regarding their participation in tax-advantaged reimbursement accounts. The impacted business owners include:

- owners of 2% or more of a Subchapter S corporation
- partners in a partnership
- members of a Limited Liability Company (LLC)

The rules affect not only the owners themselves, but certain other family members through what are known as IRS "attribution rules." These rules are designed to prevent an owner from hiring a spouse to work in the business and having the spouse participate in a tax-advantaged reimbursement account.

These owners are not allowed to participate in a Cafeteria Plan. They cannot take advantage of the tax savings associated with a Health FSA. In addition, they cannot receive tax-free reimbursement through an HRA. These owners can offer Health FSAs and HRAs to their employees, but they themselves cannot participate. These rules leave these business owners without access to two of the three tax-advantaged health reimbursement programs available to other individuals.

These owners can participate fully in an HSA program, subject to the following limitations:

- **They cannot make pre-tax payroll contributions to their HSAs.** Individuals can make such contributions only through an employer's Cafeteria Plan, and these owners cannot participate in Cafeteria Plans. They can contribute personal funds (after-tax dollars) and then deduct the contributions on their personal income tax returns. When they do so, they recoup their federal and state (if applicable) income taxes paid but not FICA payroll taxes. The impact of FICA taxes depends on their income. In 2015, the impact is 15.3% (employer and employee combined) on taxable income below $118,500, and the 2.9% Medicare levy on all income (no ceiling) above that figure.
- **They cannot receive a tax-free contribution from the business.** The business can contribute to its employees' HSAs with no tax implication to the employees, but the IRS considers any such contribution to owners to be a taxable event. *IRS Notice 2005-8, Q&A 1.*

Once these owners have established and made contributions to their HSAs, they play by the same rules as all other HSA owners. They follow the standard rules and requirements for eligibility, contribution limits, distributions, account transfers, and tax reporting.

Owners of C corporations are considered employees of the entity and generally are not subject to these restrictions. C corporations are separate and distinct entities from the owners themselves. C corporation owners own stock in the business and generally take a salary, just like other employees. They can receive employer contributions tax-free and participate in a Cafeteria Plan.

Test Your Knowledge

1. **You own a towing company organized as an LLC. You offer your employees an HSA-qualified plan and make a $1,200 annual employer contribution. You hire your husband as dispatcher. Which of the following statements is *not* true?**

   A. You can make tax-deductible employer HSA contributions to your employees' HSAs.

   B. The company can give your husband a tax-free HSA contribution because he's not an owner.

   C. You can open an HSA if you are HSA-eligible.

   D. Your husband can open an HSA if he's HSA-eligible and reimburse your eligible expenses tax-free.

2. **You are a senior partner in a law firm. Which of the following statements is true?**

   A. You cannot open your own HSA.

   B. You can receive a tax-free HSA contribution from the business.

   C. Your distributions are subject to tax and a 20% penalty.

   D. You can open an HSA if you are eligible and make tax-deductible personal contributions.

3. **Your commercial real estate venture is organized as a C corporation. Which of the following statement is *not* true?**

   A. You can make pre-tax payroll contributions to your HSA if the company has a Cafeteria Plan in place.

   B. The firm cannot give you a tax-free employer contribution.

C. You are subject to the same HSA rules as employees.

D. You can give employees a tax-free employer contribution.

TEST YOUR KNOWLEDGE ANSWERS

1. B. IRS attribution rules extend ownership of your company to your husband.
2. D. You are treated differently from others in the company only in the manner that you contribute to your HSA.
3. B. Owners of C corporations are generally treated as employees and therefore can receive the same tax-free employer contribution as other employees.

SITUATION NUMBER 4

HSAS AND RETIREMENT PLANNING

HSAs are explicitly tied to health care but also can be viewed as retirement vehicles. Because of the flexibility that HSA owners have in delaying reimbursement and maintaining balances over time (without the "use it or lose it" provision of a Health FSA), HSA owners can incorporate HSAs into their retirement planning strategy.

HSA contributions do not count against limits to contributions to qualified retirement plans. Higher-income workers and diligent savers may find themselves bumping against IRS limits to annual contributions to qualified retirement programs like traditional and Roth 401(k), 403(b) and IRA plans (as well as KEOGH, SIMPLE, and SEP programs for certain small business owners). HSA contributions do not count against those annual limits.

Because HSA owners do not lose their account balances at the end of a plan year (the concept of a "plan year" is not applicable to HSAs), unused balances remain available year after year without limit. These funds are available for future distributions. *IRS Notice 2004-2, Q&A 28.*

Accountholders can make tax-free distributions for eligible expenses later in life, even if they are no longer eligible to make

additional HSA contributions. This simple principle is one of the great benefits of an HSA. You can accumulate balances during a lifetime of contributions, then continue to make tax-free distributions later in life when you are no longer eligible to make additional contributions. *IRS Notice 2004-2, Q&A 28.*

The list of expenses eligible for tax-free distribution from an HSA in retirement expands to include certain premiums. You can make tax-free distributions to reimburse Medicare Part B (outpatient services) and Part D (prescription drug) premiums, as well as Medicare Part C (private Medicare replacement policy) premiums and most employer retirement plan premiums (not including Medex-type or Medicare Supplement plans that assume most of a participant's Medicare out-of-pocket expenses).

You can reimburse these expenses from a qualified retirement account as well. In most cases, though, your qualified retirement plan distributions are subject to ordinary income tax at the time of distribution, regardless of how the individual uses the money. By contrast, distributions for HSA-eligible expenses remain tax-free. *IRS Notice 2004-2, Q&A 27* and *IRS Notice 2004-50, Q&A 45.*

You can make distributions for non-eligible expenses as well. These distributions are subject to income tax, plus a 20% additional tax (penalty) that's waived automatically if the accountholder is age sixty-five or meets the federal tax code definition of disabled. Thus, if you make a distribution for a non-eligible expense at age sixty-five or older, distributions for non-eligible expenses face the same tax treatment as you do with distributions from a qualified retirement plan. *IRC Section 223(f)(4)(a)* and *IRS Notice 2004-2, Q&A 26.*

You can make a one-time rollover from a traditional IRA or Roth IRA to an HSA (see the Transfer section). In the case of a transfer from a traditional IRA, this transaction moves the money from an account whose distributions are taxed as ordinary income to one whose distributions for eligible expenses are tax-free. The net effect is that a $5,000 IRA might buy only $3,500 in health-related expenses after the distributions are taxed, while a $5,000 HSA will buy $5,000 of health-related services. *See IRS Notice 2008-51 and "HSA Strategy #4, "Roll over balances from an IRA to an HSA" in Part 3 for more details.*

If you do not have the financial resources to maximize contributions to a qualified retirement account and make HSA contributions, you might consider reducing your 401(k) or 403(b) contributions and channel some of that money to an HSA. This strategy makes sense only if you do not spend the funds on current expenses (thus reducing retirement savings). Example: You plan to contribute $15,000 to your 401(k) and $2,000 to your HSA. If you instead reduce your 401(k) contribution to $11,000 and increase your HSA contribution to $6,000 (with the caveat that you do not spend the additional $4,000 on current expenses), you save the same $15,000 for retirement. In the unlikely event that you do not have any medical expenses for tax-free spending in retirement, the money in the HSA can be used with the same tax treatment as the 401(k) savings after age 65. *See "HSA Strategy #5, "Divert qualified retirement plan contributions to your HSA" in Part 3 for more details.*

If you plan to maintain and build HSA balances for retirement, you should keep receipts for all HSA-eligible expenses that you could have reimbursed but did not reimburse through your HSA. You can reimburse these expenses at any time in the future. If you are audited at that time, you may need to prove that you spent at least an equal amount over the years since you established your HSA on eligible medical expenses. Example: You accumulate HSA balances for twenty years by not reimbursing eligible expenses. At retirement (or earlier), if you need cash for any reason, you can make a tax-free distribution from your HSA by reimbursing all those expenses that you could have reimbursed, but did not, at the time of service. *IRS Notice 2004-2, Q&A 28.*

TEST YOUR KNOWLEDGE

1. **Which of the following statements is/are true?**

    A. You can reduce your 401(k) contributions to fund your HSA, but your combined 401(k) and HSA contributions cannot exceed the 401(k) maximum contribution for that year.

    B. You can roll over funds from an IRA, SIMPLE, or SEP plan into an HSA but not balances from a 401(k) or 403(b) plan.

    C. If you have a positive HSA balance, you must reimburse a medical expense from an HSA rather than from a qualified retirement plan.

    D. You can make a one-time rollover from a traditional IRA or Roth IRA to an HSA.

2. **Which of the following statements is/are true?**

    A. At age sixty-five, you can make distributions for non-eligible expenses without paying taxes or penalties.

    B. At age sixty-five, but not before, you can begin to reimburse your spouse's Medicare premiums tax-free.

    C. At age sixty-five, but not before, you can begin to pay your spouse's Medicare deductibles and copays.

    D. At age sixty-five, you are no longer eligible to contribute to an HSA.

3. **Which of the following expenses is/are *not* eligible for tax-free reimbursement from an HSA?**

    A. Your thirty-year-old disabled daughter's Medicare B premium if you have not reached age sixty-five.

B. Your wife's Medicare deductible, if you have not reached age sixty-five.

C. Your dental services not covered by insurance if you have not yet reached age sixty-five.

D. Your thirty-year-old disabled daughter's doctor's visit subject to Medicare Part B deductible.

TEST YOUR KNOWLEDGE ANSWERS

1. D. Your HSA contributions are independent of qualified retirement plan limits, you cannot roll funds from a SIMPLE IRA or SEP IRA into an HSA, and you are not restricted in your distributions from an HSA or qualified retirement plan.

2. B. You never escape the tax consequences of making a distribution for a non-eligible expense, you can pay your spouse's eligible expenses (except Medicare premiums) before you turn age sixty-five, and you do not lose HSA eligibility at age sixty-five unless you enroll in Medicare.

3. A. You cannot reimburse anyone's Medicare premiums until you, the accountholder, turn age sixty-five. You can, however, reimburse any eligible non-premium expenses incurred by an eligible recipient before you turn age sixty-five.

SITUATION NUMBER 5

HSAS AND CHILDREN

Children who are your tax dependents are not eligible to open their own HSAs. If your child qualifies as a tax dependent under Section 152 of the IRC, that child cannot establish his or her own HSA. However, you can reimburse your dependent child's eligible expenses tax-free from your HSA. *IRC Section 223(b)(6)* and *IRS Notice 2004-2, Q&A 2.*

You remain HSA-eligible even if your children are covered by Medicare (in the case of disability) or Medicaid or other disqualifying coverage, including a spouse's or ex-spouse's non-HSA-qualified plan. Medicare and Medicaid issue individual policies only. Your child or children may be enrolled in these programs without impacting your ability to remain HSA-eligible and make full contributions to your HSA since you are not entitled to benefits through their Medicare or Medicaid coverage. The same holds true for their coverage under another commercial health plan that is not an HSA-qualified plan, as long as you are not entitled to benefits under that plan. *IRS Notice 2004-2, Q&A 2* and *IRS Notice 2008-59, Q&A 11.*

If you cover more than one person on your health plan, you can contribute up to the family maximum, even if the only other covered individuals are children who are not HSA-

eligible. Your contribution amount is governed by the number of individuals enrolled on your health insurance contract. So even if you are a single parent covering two dependent children who are not HSA-eligible, you can make a full family contribution (if otherwise eligible to do so) because of your children's coverage through your health insurance, even though they are not HSA-eligible. *IRC Section 223(c)(4)* and *IRS Notice 2008-59, Q&A 16.*

You can reimburse your dependent child's eligible expenses tax free from your HSA even if the child is not covered on your health insurance contract. You can reimburse tax-free the eligible expenses that your spouse and dependents incur, whether or not they are covered on your health plan. The rules governing HSA distributions are based on the individual's relationship to you, not that person's health insurance coverage. *IRS Notice 2004-50, Q&A 36.*

You cannot reimburse your child's expenses tax-free from your HSA if the child is no longer your tax dependent. Children are allowed to remain on their parent's health insurance until their twenty-sixth birthday in most cases under a provision of the Affordable Care Act. However, that provision does not extend to HSAs because these accounts are not health plans. HSAs are governed by federal tax law, not federal insurance laws, and federal tax law says that an accountholder cannot reimburse expenses incurred by a non-eligible individual tax-free. *IRC Section 223(b) (6)* and *IRS Notice 2004-2, Q&A 2.*

If your child is not your tax dependent and remains on your health plan to age twenty-six, that child can establish his or her own HSA if otherwise HSA-eligible. Your child who's no longer a tax dependent but is covered on your health plan and is otherwise HSA-eligible can open his or her own HSA. Anyone, including you, can contribute to that HSA, though the child receives the tax deduction. And the child can reimburse his or her eligible expenses tax-free from that HSA. *IRC Section 223(c)(1)(A).*

An adult child can contribute to his or her own HSA at the family level if he or she remains covered on your family health insurance policy. Section 223 and subsequent IRS notices and rulings have not dealt with the presence of two or more adults who are not married on an HSA-qualified insurance contract. The issue is moot if the child has his or her own policy but very relevant as long as he or she remains covered on your plan and you are contributing to an HSA too.

A conservative approach would be to make sure that the sum of the contributions from all family members to their personal HSAs does not exceed the statutory maximum contribution for a family contract. However, to maximize total contributions to the HSAs, you might want to discuss with your personal legal or tax counsel whether you can make a full family contribution to each HSA owned by an HSA-eligible individual covered on the contract. Many experts now confidently advise that since the adult child is covered by a family contract, he or she can contribute at the family level.

Test Your Knowledge

1. **Your twenty-four-year-old child remains covered on your health plan while completing graduate school. Which of the following statements is true?**

   A. As long as he remains your tax dependent, you can reimburse his expenses tax-free from your HSA.

   B. Either you can reimburse his expenses tax-free, or he can set up his own HSA to reimburse the expenses tax-free.

   C. If he's still your tax dependent, he can set up his own HSA to reimburse the expenses tax-free, or you can reimburse them subject to tax and penalties.

D. Neither you nor he can reimburse these expenses tax-free if he's no longer your tax dependent.

2. **Your twenty-five-year-old daughter is pursuing an acting career and living independently in California while remaining on your health insurance to reduce her living costs and files her own taxes. What's true about her dental expenses?**

   A. You can reimburse them tax-free from your HSA because she's covered on your insurance.
   B. You cannot reimburse her expenses tax-free because she's not your tax dependent.
   C. You can reimburse her expenses tax-free, but you'll pay a 20% penalty.
   D. She can set up and fund her own HSA, but if you contribute to her HSA, she cannot reimburse the expenses tax-free.

3. **Which of the following individual's expenses can you *not* reimburse tax-free from your HSA?**

   A. Your disabled daughter's, if she's also enrolled in Medicare.
   B. Your stepson's, if he's enrolled in Medicaid rather than on your health plan.
   C. Your pre-teen son's, if he's covered on his mother's non-HSA-qualified plan.
   D. Your daughter's, if she's no longer a tax dependent.

4. **Who can open his or her own HSA to reimburse his or her own eligible expenses tax-free?**

   A. Your son who's living independently two states away and working in construction but remains enrolled on your HSA-qualified plan.

    B. Your disabled son who remains your tax dependent.

    C. Your daughter who's in graduate school but dependent on you for tuition, living expenses, and health insurance coverage.

    D. Your teenage stepson who lives with you and your wife.

TEST YOUR KNOWLEDGE ANSWERS

1. A. As long as he's your tax dependent, you can reimburse his expenses, and he cannot open his own HSA. Under no circumstances can a parent OR child reimburse the same expense tax-free.

2. B. You cannot reimburse her expenses tax-free because she's not your tax dependent. She can open her own HSA and reimburse her own eligible expenses tax-free, regardless of whether you give her the money to fund her account.

3. D. You can reimburse your tax dependents' eligible expenses tax-free. Only the daughter who's no longer your tax dependent is not eligible for tax-free distributions from your HSA (but she can set up her own if otherwise HSA-eligible).

4. A. The others are all your tax dependents, and individuals who can be claimed as someone else's tax dependents are not eligible to open their own HSAs.

SITUATION NUMBER 6

HSAS AND DOMESTIC PARTNERS

The biggest recent change in HSAs was the June 2015 Supreme Court decision granting the right of same-sex couples to marry nationwide following their earlier decision striking down the Defense of Marriage Act of 1996 provision that a marriage is a state-sanctioned union between a man and a woman. Going forward under most aspects of federal tax law including the application of those provisions to HSAs, a state-recognized marriage is a marriage. The federal tax code does not recognize other relationships, however. Chief among them is domestic partners.

These individuals, even though they may be covered on the health plan, are not treated as spouses for HSA purposes. This different treatment creates some opportunities and places some restrictions on these individuals' actions and the tax consequences of certain actions.

In most areas of life, this different treatment results in less flexibility and perhaps less benefit for these relationships. In at least one important area, though, HSAs create an opportunity that other tax-advantaged reimbursement accounts do not.

You cannot reimburse your domestic partner's expenses tax-free from your HSA unless that individual qualifies in another

way (such as being your tax dependent due to disability). You can cover your domestic partner on your health insurance if your employer, your insurer, and state law allow, but you cannot reimburse his or her eligible expense tax-free from your HSA unless he or she is your tax dependent (which is rare). Any distributions from your HSA to cover a domestic partner's eligible expenses are included in your taxable income (and subject to a 20% penalty if you are under age sixty-five and not disabled).

You generally cannot reimburse your domestic partner's children's eligible expenses, whether or not they are covered on your health plan. The only exception is if your domestic partner's child is your tax dependent, an infrequent situation that might occur if your domestic partner is your tax dependent, for example, due to disability.

If you are covered on a family contract, you can contribute up to the family maximum, even if your domestic partner is not HSA-eligible. The size of the contract (covering only one person, or multiple people) determines your contribution amount, without regard to whether anyone else covered on the insurance plan is HSA-eligible or eligible to receive tax-free reimbursements from your HSA. *IRS Notice 2008-59, Q&A 16.*

If your domestic partner is otherwise HSA-eligible, he or she can open an HSA to reimburse his or her own (and dependents') expenses tax-free. Since an individual does not have to be the health plan subscriber to be HSA-eligible, your domestic partner can open his or her own HSA to reimburse his or her eligible expenses tax-free, plus any eligible expenses that his or her tax dependents incur. In this scenario, you can reimburse your own and your tax dependents' eligible expenses tax-free, your domestic partner can reimburse his or her own (and tax dependents') eligible expenses tax-free, and each of you generally can reimburse your own child's/children's expenses from your personal HSAs as well.

This concept is important. Your domestic partner's (as well as his or her tax dependents') eligible expenses are not reimbursable through your Health FSA or an HRA unless your domestic partner is your tax dependent, which is rare. Those reimbursement plans are employer-based, and only the employee can be a subscriber. By contrast, HSAs are individual reimbursement accounts, and more than one individual covered on the contract can qualify to open an account and reimburse his or her own (and tax dependents') eligible expenses. In this respect, an HSA extends to nontraditional families an opportunity that they would not have if they participated in another tax-advantaged reimbursement account.

If you and your domestic partner are covered on a family contract and you both open and contribute to HSAs, you can both contribute at the family level. Section 223 of the Internal Revenue Code and subsequent IRS interpretations address contribution limits only for married couples. It does not prescribe what happens when two adults who are not married are covered on a health insurance contract.

The most conservative approach is to contribute no more than the maximum family contribution to all HSAs combined. A growing number of HSA trustees and attorneys advise clients that each individual can open an HSA and that each can contribute up to the maximum HSA contribution for a family contract.

The rules for married same-sex couples are the same as for any other married couple. There may be a large number of same-sex couples who were married in another state and that marriage was not recognized in their own state until the June 2015 Supreme Court ruling. These people will now need to limit their contributions in their individual account to the family limit like any other married couple, although they may distribute the family limit between the two accounts in any manner they choose.

TEST YOUR KNOWLEDGE

1. **You want to cover your domestic partner on your health insurance. Which of the following statements is true?**

   A. You can cover your domestic partner, but any insurance payments to providers for your partner's expenses will be taxable to your spouse.

   B. You can cover your domestic partner if you petition a family court and demonstrate a financial commitment (joint ownership of financial assets and/or real estate).

   C. You cannot cover your domestic partner under any circumstances.

   D. You can cover your domestic partner if state law, your employer, and your insurer permit such coverage.

2. **Your domestic partner incurs a major deductible expense while covered on your health plan. Which of the following statements is true?**

   A. You can reimburse the expense tax-free from your HSA since the expense applies to the deductible on your health plan.

   B. You cannot reimburse the expense tax-free from your HSA under any circumstances, even if he or she is your tax dependent.

   C. You can reimburse the expense from your HSA, and the distribution will be included in your taxable income, but the 20% penalty is waived.

   D. Your domestic partner, if otherwise eligible, can open his or her own HSA from which he or she can reimburse the expense tax-free.

3. **Your domestic partner is your tax dependent due to a disability. She's also covered by Medicare. What is true of her expenses?**

    A. You can reimburse all her eligible expenses tax-free from your HSA only if Medicare does not reimburse any portion of them.

    B. You can reimburse her financial responsibility for eligible expenses tax-free from your HSA.

    C. You cannot reimburse these expenses from your HSA.

    D. You can reimburse a portion of these expenses tax-free from your HSA, but since she's your domestic partner, the 20% penalty applies.

TEST YOUR KNOWLEDGE ANSWERS

1. D. Your domestic partner's eligibility to enroll on your health insurance contract is a function of state law and your employer's and health plan's eligibility criteria.

2. D. You cannot reimburse your domestic partner's eligible expense tax-free from your HSA unless that individual is your tax dependent. Otherwise, any distributions from your HSA for your domestic partner's expenses are included in your taxable income and subject to a 20% penalty (the penalty applies if you are under age sixty-five and not disabled).

3. B. Her Medicare coverage is irrelevant since she's already your tax dependent and therefore not eligible to open her own HSA. You can reimburse her expenses not paid by other sources tax-free from your HSA because she's your tax dependent.

SITUATION NUMBER 7

HSAS AND DIVORCE

It is important to distinguish between a former spouse's right to remain on your health plan and your ability to reimburse that individual's HSA-eligible expenses tax-free. Under a divorce decree (or court order of separate maintenance prior to a divorce), the court may require you to provide health insurance for your spouse. If state law, your employer, and your insurer allow it, you can cover this individual on your policy. Otherwise, you may have to purchase and pay for a policy for this individual.

Regardless of how the court handles the issue of coverage, federal tax law dictates how your HSA works.

You cannot reimburse tax-free your ex-spouse's expenses (or expenses incurred by your separated spouse under a court order of separate maintenance). Whether your former spouse is covered on your health plan is not relevant to tax-free reimbursement from your HSA. Any expenses that you reimburse from your HSA with dates of service after the divorce decree or court order of separate maintenance are included in your taxable income, and a 20% penalty applies if you are under age sixty-five and not disabled.

You generally can reimburse your dependent children's expenses, whether or not you have legal custody or they are

covered on your health plan. You are allowed to reimburse tax-free expenses incurred by children of your former marriage, as long as they live with either of you for more than half the year, you and your ex-spouse together provide at least half their support and you have a decree of divorce or separate maintenance in place. *IRS Publication 502, "Child of divorced or separated parents" on page 4 of the 2012 edition.*

You generally can reimburse your dependent children's expenses, even if they are not covered on your health plan. If your ex-spouse maintains health insurance coverage for your dependent children, you can still reimburse their eligible expenses tax-free from your HSA. The fact that they are not enrolled on your health plan is not relevant—just as it is not relevant prior to the divorce. *IRS Notice 2004-50, Q&A 36* and *IRS Notice 2008-59, Q&A 33.*

If you are covered on a family contract, you can contribute up to the family maximum, even if your ex-spouse is not HSA-eligible. The size of the contract (covering only one person or multiple people) determines your contribution level, without regard to whether anyone else covered on the insurance plan is HSA-eligible. *IRS Notice 2008-59, Q&A 16.*

If your ex-spouse is otherwise HSA-eligible, he or she can open an HSA to reimburse eligible personal expenses tax-free. Since an individual does not have to be the health plan subscriber, your ex-spouse can open his or her own HSA to reimburse his or her eligible expenses tax-free. In this scenario, you can reimburse your own expenses tax-free, your ex-spouse can reimburse his or her own expenses tax-free, and either of you generally can reimburse your child's expenses from your personal HSAs as well.

This concept is important. You cannot reimburse an ex-spouse's expenses through a Health FSA or an HRA under any circumstances. These reimbursement plans are employer-based, and only the employee can be a subscriber. By contrast, HSAs are individual reimbursement accounts, and more than one family member can qualify to open an account and reimburse his or her expenses. In this respect, an HSA extends to ex-spouses an opportunity that they would not have if you subscribed to another tax-advantaged reimbursement account.

If you and your ex-spouse are covered on a family contract and you both open and contribute to HSAs, both of you can contribute up to the family maximum. The law addresses contribution limits only for married couples. The law does not directly address divorce (and certain other situations including domestic partners). The most conservative position, which certainly would pass IRS scrutiny, is to contribute to the multiple HSAs no more than the family contract maximum.

A growing number of HSA trustees and attorneys are advising clients that each individual can open an HSA and that each can contribute up to the maximum HSA contribution for a family contract.

HSA assets may be included in divorce settlements. An HSA is an asset owned by one individual. In a divorce settlement, assets are distributed between two parties. It would not be unusual for a spouse to ask for a portion of the other spouse's HSA balances to provide a cushion to reimburse his or her future HSA-eligible expenses until he or she can begin to fund his or her own HSA. In this case, a transfer of assets from one HSA to another would not constitute a distribution subject to taxes and penalties. *IRC Section 227(f)(7).*

TEST YOUR KNOWLEDGE

1. **You and your wife entered into a decree of separate maintenance on June 23, 2014. What's true of her MRI with a date of service of May 30, 2014?**

   A. You cannot reimburse it tax-free from your HSA unless you pay it before June 23.

B. You can reimburse it tax-free from your HSA at any point in the future, since you were legally married at the time of the expense.

C. You can reimburse it tax-free, but the 20% penalty applies.

D. Your reimbursement is included in your taxable income, but the 20% penalty is waived as long as you reimburse within a year of the decree of separate maintenance.

2. **Your two children live with your ex-spouse in another part of the country. What's generally true about their expenses?**

A. In most cases, you can reimburse their eligible expenses that you pay tax-free from your HSA.

B. You can reimburse them tax-free only if the divorce decree says you are required to pay them.

C. You cannot reimburse them tax-free from your HSA unless you declare them as tax dependents on your federal income tax return.

D. You can reimburse them, and the reimbursement will be included in your taxable income, but the 20% penalty is waived.

3. **Your ex-wife is covered on your health insurance by court order. Which of the following statements is true?**

A. You can reimburse her eligible expenses tax-free from your HSA because she's covered on your health plan.

B. You can reimburse her eligible expenses tax-free only if the divorce decree requires you to do so.

C. You cannot reimburse her eligible expenses tax-free because she's not an eligible recipient as an ex-spouse.

D. You can reimburse her expenses, but the distribution will be included in her taxable income, and she'll pay an additional 20% penalty.

4. **Which of the following statements is true about your ex-spouse's HSA-eligible expenses?**

A. You can reimburse these expenses through any tax-advantaged reimbursement account, but reimbursements through a Health FSA or HRA are included the distribution in your taxable income, and you pay an additional 20% penalty.

B. You can reimburse them tax-free through a Health FSA or HRA but not an HSA.

C. You cannot reimburse them tax-free from your HSA, but your ex-spouse may be able to open an HSA to reimburse the expenses tax-free.

D. You can reimburse them through a Health FSA, HRA, and HSA, but the distribution would not be tax-free and may be subject to a 10% penalty.

Test Your Knowledge Answers

1. B. There is no time limit on distributions, and there are no circumstances prior to the accountholder's turning age sixty-five or being declared disabled when an expense would be subject to either taxation or the penalty, but not both.

2. A. Reimbursements are governed by tax law, not court orders. And in the special case of divorce, in most situations, either parent can reimburse some or all eligible expenses tax-free from his or her HSA.

3. C. Because she's not an eligible recipient of reimbursements from your HSA under federal tax rules, any distributions are subject to income tax and a 20% penalty. A divorce degree does not override federal tax law.

4. C. You cannot reimburse an ex-spouse's eligible expenses through a Health FSA or HRA. You can reimburse them through your HSA, but the expenses are subject to income tax and a 20% penalty, the same treatment as any other distributions for a non-eligible expense. Your ex-spouse, if otherwise HSA-eligible, can open an HSA to reimburse his or her eligible expenses on tax-free basis.

SITUATION NUMBER 8

HSAS AND DEATH

You name a designated beneficiary when you open your HSA and can change the beneficiary at any time. An HSA is a trust, and all trusts have beneficiaries. During your lifetime, you are the beneficiary. Upon your death, your HSA passes to your designated beneficiary (or is included in your estate, if you fail to name a beneficiary). *IRS Notice 2004-2, Q&A 31* and *IRS Publication 969 (page 11 in the 2012 edition).*

Your HSA passes to your husband or wife if you name your spouse as beneficiary. If you name your federally recognized spouse as your designated beneficiary, your HSA passes to your spouse outside the estate. It remains an HSA, and your spouse enjoys all the benefits and accepts all the responsibility of managing the HSA. Your spouse may have never been covered by an HSA-qualified plan but can now use the HSA to cover any qualified expense for the new owner, any new spouse, and any current tax dependents even if they cannot add any new money to the account. Your spouse then designates a beneficiary to receive the assets in the event of his or her death. *IRC Section 223(f)(8) (A)* and *IRS Notice 2004-2, Q&A 31.*

If you name anyone else as your designated beneficiary, the HSA ceases to be an HSA as of the date of your death. Your HSA trustee liquidates the assets in the HSA, and your designated beneficiary receives the fair market value of the assets. This distribution is included in the recipient's taxable income in the year of the distribution. *IRC Section 223(f)(B)(i)* and *IRS Notice 2004-2, Q&A 31.*

Your HSA can continue to pay your eligible expenses after your death. Your survivors can reimburse any unreimbursed eligible expenses that you incurred from the date that you established your HSA. These distributions must be made within one year of your death and go to the survivors entirely tax-free since those expenses could have been withdrawn tax-free by the deceased before death. *IRC Section 223(f)(B)(ii)* and *IRS Notice 2004-2, Q&A 31.*

TEST YOUR KNOWLEDGE

1. **Who can be a designated beneficiary of your HSA?**
   - A. Your spouse only.
   - B. Anyone whose expenses you could reimburse tax-free from your HSA prior to your death.
   - C. Anyone.
   - D. No one. Your HSA is liquidated upon your death and included in your estate.

2. **What happens when you name your federally recognized spouse as your designated beneficiary?**
   - A. Your HSA passes to your spouse, who assumes control and uses the HSA as if he or she had been the original owner.
   - B. The HSA is liquidated, and the proceeds are taxable to your spouse.

C. Your spouse has to pay income taxes on the value of the HSA, after which he or she can continue to use it as an HSA.

D. Your spouse has the option to split the HSA and give a piece to each of your surviving children as their own HSAs within a year of your death.

3. **Your heirs find $2,000 in eligible expenses that you did not reimburse during your lifetime. What can they do?**

A. It is too late to reimburse the expenses once you have died.

B. They can make tax-free distributions to reimburse any eligible expenses that you incurred during your lifetime. The distributions are taxable to your estate, but no 20% penalty applies.

C. They can reimburse your funeral expenses under a special provision of the law for eligible expenses for decedent accountholders.

D. They can reimburse your eligible expenses tax-free within one year of your death.

TEST YOUR KNOWLEDGE ANSWERS

1. C. You can name anyone as your designated beneficiary, but the HSA is treated differently depending on whether the designated beneficiary is your legal spouse or someone else.

2. A. When the spouse inherits an HSA, it is a straightforward, nontaxable event.

3. D. Your heirs have one year after your death to reimburse your eligible expenses.

Situation Number 9

HSAs by State

Most HSA rules and regulations are set at the national level by the IRS. In a federal republic, states sometimes alter the rules as they pertain to their individual state residents, but cannot change the federal rules for their state's citizens.

Some states define income differently than the IRS. As a result, some income that may be tax free at the federal level may not be at the state level. The federal government does not tax qualified HSA contributions, distributions and rollovers from an Archer MSA to an HSA, but some states do. While these state laws are not necessarily a barrier to offering HSAs, such state laws could be considered a disincentive to having one.

All but a few states now conform to the Federal Internal Revenue Code for HSA purposes. Only Alabama, California, and New Jersey do not offer tax free contributions at the state level as of 2015.

We have provided the link to the state's revenue department for more information.

- Alabama: http://www.ador.state.al.us
- California: http://www.ftb.ca.gov

- New Jersey: http://www.state.nj.us/treasury/taxation/index.htm

As of 2015, two states have no income tax but do tax dividends and interest. HSA holders may have to pay taxes on any interest or dividends earned in their HSA. These states are as follows:

- New Hampshire
- Tennessee

PART 3
HSA STRATEGIES

Up to this point, we've focused on HSA rules around eligibility, contributions, distributions, and transfers. We've reviewed specific situations in which you may find yourself, such as the owner of a business organized in a certain way, a worker who's no longer covered by an HSA-qualified plan or a retiree.

This section builds on that knowledge. We focus on specific ways that you can maximize the value of your HSA. It is important to understand these strategies when you first become HSA-eligible since many of them allow you to reap benefits years into the future if you know how to act now.

As with qualified retirement plans and other tax-favored accounts, individuals who know very little but just participate can reap some tax benefits. On the other hand, individuals who take their knowledge to the next level can experience many times the tax savings and degree of financial freedom because they understand how to make these accounts work for them as part of their overall financial strategy.

In this section, we review strategies that allow you to turbo-charge your tax savings and account balances. Each strategy by itself, if you apply it to your particular situation, can increase your tax savings and personal wealth accumulation. Some of these strategies, when used in concert, will take you to an even higher financial plane.

Buckle your seat belts, open your mind and learn how to make your HSA work for you to create a more prosperous financial future.

Strategy Number 1

Consider a Limited-Purpose Health FSA

You might want to consider contributing to two reimbursement accounts.

If you buy group insurance through your employer, it may make sense to participate in a Limited-Purpose Health FSA in addition to making contributions to your HSA. As you may recall from the chapter on *Eligibility*, a Limited-Purpose Health FSA limits reimbursement to dental, vision, and preventive care expenses (many of which are now covered in full under provisions of the Affordable Care Act). All these expenses (and many others) are eligible for reimbursement through your HSA.

The Benefits of a Limited-Purpose Health FSA

So why might it make sense to make an election to a Limited-Purpose Health FSA?

You maximize your tax savings. Every dollar of salary that you elect to defer into an FSA reduces your taxable income dollar-for-dollar. If you are likely to incur dental or vision expenses and you plan to make a full HSA contribution in 2016 ($3,350 for a self-only and $6,750 for a family contract), you can make an additional election into your employer's Limited-Purpose Health FSA up to your employer's limit (not to exceed $2,550 in 2015, a figure adjusted for inflation in subsequent years). A Limited-Purpose Health FSA election of $2,000 reduces your taxable income by $2,000, resulting in (roughly) $500 tax savings. That's $500 you'd otherwise pay in federal and state taxes that you instead can spend on eligible expenses.

You maximize your HSA balance. If your goal is to maximize your balances in your HSA, you want to contribute as much as possible and distribute as little as possible while still maximizing your tax benefits. You can use your Limited-Purpose Health FSA election to pay for dental, vision, and preventive services that you'd otherwise be able to reimburse tax-free only by dipping further into your HSA balance (thus limiting the HSA balance that you could retain to reimburse future expenses, for example in retirement).

You manage cash flow. If you have a large dental, vision, or preventive care expense early in the plan year (common examples include a root canal and crown, orthodontics, and vision correction surgery), you can access your full Limited-Purpose Health FSA election immediately, while you cannot spend HSA funds that you have not contributed yet. Thus, the Limited-Purpose Health FSA offers cash flow advantages above its additional tax savings.

ISSUES AROUND LIMITED-PURPOSE HEALTH FSAS

The Limited-Purpose Health FSA strategy is not risk-free. First, your employer must offer this option. An employer might be reluctant to offer the program for several reasons:

- Elections to general and Limited-Purpose Health FSA are subject to "uniform coverage." This term refers to your ability to spend the entire election at any time during the plan year. You make equal payments through pay-roll deduction to cover your reimbursements. If you leave employment having spent more than your employer has collected through pre-tax payroll contributions, your employer cannot bill you for the difference. An employer therefore has the potential risk of losing money (though such a loss may be offset by balances that other partici-pants forfeit if they do not spend their entire elections before the end of the plan year).

- Employers absorb administrative costs of offering a Health FSA. Employers typically contract with a third party that administers the program. The third party gen-erally charges an annual fixed fee and a monthly admin-istrative fee per account. These fees are often in the range of about $60 to $80 per year. Employers do not have to pay federal payroll taxes on their employees' Health FSA elections. The breakeven point for an employer is about $1,000. In other words, the payroll tax savings on the first $1,000 of a participant's election pays the annual admin-istrative fee for that Health FSA account.

- A Limited-Purpose Health FSA is another account that an employer has to administer. It takes resources to man-age the program, present it at open enrollment, introduce new employees to the option, and explain to participants why they cannot change their elections during the year unless they experience a qualified event like marriage, divorce, birth, adoption, or death. While there is some employer effort involved, the third-party administra-tor assumes responsibility for most of the work—issu-ing debit cards and tracking charges, processing manual claims, updating employee balances, and providing cus-tomer service when employees have a question or issue.

- Under a provision of the Affordable Care Act, you can-not elect to contribute more than $2,550 to a general or Limited-Purpose Health FSA, beginning with plan years commencing on or after January 1, 2015 (though your employer can choose a lower limit). This provision limits your total tax savings via Health FSA elections. In most cases, though, $2,550 is an adequate amount to cover dental, vision, and preventive care expenses.

The other party at risk with a Health FSA is you, the participant. Elections to a Limited-Purpose Health FSA, like elections to a general Health FSA, are subject to the "use it or lose it" rule that gives pause to many potential participants and prompts many actual participants to underfund their Health FSAs. Participants forfeit any unused balances (or if their employer elects an October 2013 change to the rules, any balances greater than up to $500). The forfeited money is returned to the employer, who by law cannot return the money to participating employees in the proportion that they forfeit it. Instead, employers typically retain participants' forfeited balances to offset the administrative costs of hiring a third party to run the Health FSA program.

So the risk to you is simple. You can keep unlimited balances in your HSA for future use. By contrast, you forfeit unused Health FSA balances, unless your employer allows an unlimited rollover for a limited period (the 2½-month grace period) or a limited rollover for an unlimited period (rollover of up to $500). In either case, the rollover is far more limited than your options with an HSA.

If you are not sure whether you are going to have enough dental, vision, or preventive care expenses to spend your entire Limited-Purpose Health FSA election, you are better off contributing those dollars to your HSA. After all, you realize the same tax savings either way, and you can reimburse those expenses out of either account, but you retain unspent funds in your HSA and risk forfeit unused balances in your Limited-Purpose Health FSA.

Do not let this fear of forfeited elections scare you into inaction when action represents a financial opportunity. Here's a simple example: You elect to contribute $1,600 to your Limited-Purpose Health FSA, which does not include a grace period or a limited rollover. You have some restorative dental work ($900) done early in the year and then order two new pairs of prescription glasses ($500) late in the year. You do not spend the final $200 of your balance. You really have not lost $200, though. With an election of $1,600, you saved about $400 in taxes if you are in the 25% tax bracket. So the $200 that you forfeited is money that you would have paid in taxes. Your only loss is an opportunity loss—the opportunity to spend $200 more. You paid $1,200 (net) to receive only $1,400 of benefit, rather than the full $1,600 to which you were entitled.

As with any financial decision, you need to weigh carefully the benefits and costs of participating in a particular program. If you do not plan to maximize your HSA contributions, you are probably better off making additional HSA contributions to reimburse eligible dental, vision, and preventive care services. If you expect to have major dental or vision expenses early in the year before you are able to front-load contributions to your HSA, a Limited-Purpose Health FSA election provides you with access to your entire election immediately and erases the risk that you'll forfeit all or a portion of your unused balance at the end of the year.

Advantages of this strategy:

- You can extend your tax advantage beyond what is allowed in an HSA alone.
- You can maximize the HSA balance that you carry into the future while reimbursing current tax-free eligible dental, vision and preventive care services.
- You can gain a cash-flow advantage by accessing Limited-Purpose Health FSA elections at any time during the plan year.

Disadvantages of this strategy:

- You risk forfeiting unused Limited-Purpose Health FSA balances. Your employer may minimize this risk by (1) including a 2½-month grace period during which you can continue to purchase items eligible for reimbursement or (2) allowing a rollover of up to $500 into the following year's plan.

Strategy Number 2

Delay Reimbursements and Save Receipts

There is no deadline for reimbursing eligible expenses tax-free from your HSA. This can be one of the most powerful aspects of the HSA.

By contrast, you must claim any reimbursements from a Health FSA or HRA within the current plan year (including a claims run-out period that generally ends three months after the end of the plan year).

Here's how to make this provision in the law work for you: Maximize your HSA contributions and treat your HSA like an IRA that turns today's medical expenses into tax-free withdrawals for any purpose, anytime in the future. If you pay small eligible expenses from your personal funds, you'll retain HSA balances, which continue to grow tax-free. The higher your balance, the more funds you'll have to grow and spend in the future.

When to Adopt This Strategy

Expenses you pay today and leave in your HSA can be used anytime for any purpose. You have effectively created a tax-free fund for the future, regardless of your tax bracket.

If you save money now and do not have current expenses, even if you believe that you'll have less income in retirement, you'll appreciate the ability to reimburse eligible expenses tax-free from an HSA. And do not think you will not have such expenses. Fidelity Investments conducts an annual survey of how much a couple age sixty-five covered by traditional Medicare (Parts A, B, and D) will spend out of pocket on health care during the remainder of their lives if they retired that year. The 2014 figure, released in June 2014, is $220,000, including Medicare premiums and expenses for medical, dental, and vision, as well as over-the-counter items. Assuming an effective tax rate of, conservatively, 25% (state and federal income and payroll taxes), you would have to save $293,333 in a qualified retirement account that taxes all distributions as ordinary income to pay those $220,000 in expenses. By contrast, you can reimburse the same $220,000 in eligible expenses from an HSA—with the same tax treatment of contributions and account balance growth—with a total of $220,000 in distributions. This strategy leaves you with an additional $73,333—which you'd otherwise lose in taxes—to finance your retirement and spend on your priorities rather than the governments'.

If you believe that you'll face higher taxes in retirement, this strategy makes sense as well. The traditional thinking is that individuals pay lower taxes in retirement because they have lower incomes. This thinking may cost you money, however.

First, in retirement, you may face mandatory annual distribution amounts from your qualified retirement accounts that exceed your needs for that year. Those distributions, usually beginning at age seventy and a half, are taxed as ordinary income. You cannot escape these mandatory minimum distributions in many qualified retirement accounts, regardless of your financial needs in a particular year.

Second, in retirement you may lose a number of deductions that reduce your taxable income during your working years. Those deductions include the home mortgage deduction (if you own your home free and clear in retirement), deduction of business expenses (if you are self-employed in a primary or secondary job and deduct your home office, vehicle, travel, phone, computer, and other items necessary to run your business), and perhaps charitable contributions (if money is tighter or the uncertainty of future expenses leaves you more conservative in your annual giving).

Third, given the run-up of the federal debt during the past decade, states' unfunded public employee pension responsibilities, and the full financial impact of implementation of the Affordable Care Act, it is quite possible that marginal income tax rates will rise above current levels to meet these obligations.

If any of these trends impacts you, you may be better off paying current expenses with today's after-tax dollars and preserving your HSA balances to pay expenses tax-free for future eligible expenses in a higher-tax environment.

THE FLEXIBILITY OF THIS STRATEGY

What happens if your HSA balances are so high *in retirement* that you cannot possibly spend the money on eligible expenses only? Though this scenario is unlikely for most Americans (think back to Fidelity's $220,000 retirement health care figure), it is not a problem. Under current law, once you turn age sixty-five, distributions from a qualified retirement plan and distributions from an HSA for non-eligible expenses receive the same tax treatment: They are included in taxable income, but no penalty applies. You generally can begin to make distributions without penalty (10%) from a qualified retirement plan at age fifty-nine and a half, while you cannot begin to make distributions for non-eligible HSA expenses without penalty (20%) until age sixty-five (or earlier if you meet the IRS definition of disabled, as defined in IRC Section 72(m)(7)).

What happens if you need to access your HSA balances *before retirement?* Again, not a problem. As long as you save the receipts for those eligible expenses that you could have reimbursed tax-free from your HSA, but did not, you can reimburse those expenses tax-free at any point in the future. For example, you need a quick infusion of cash to pay some unexpected car repairs, have fallen a little short of paying your granddaughter's tuition for her final semester of nursing school, or need to replace the heating or air conditioning system in your home. You can make a tax-free withdrawal for any of these expenses—even though they are not HSA-eligible expenses—from your HSA with no taxes or penalties as long as you've retained receipts for expenses that you incurred since you established your HSA that you could have reimbursed from your HSA but did not.

And when you adopt this strategy of consciously retaining balances to reimburse eligible expenses tax-free in retirement, you can change your approach at any time. You are not locked into deferring reimbursement anywhere but in your own mind. For example, if you are diligent about maximizing your account balance for future distributions and then face a high eligible expense, nothing prevents you from reimbursing that expense from your HSA tax-free and then continuing to reimburse other expenses with personal funds to build your HSA balances.

Note: An alternative to making this one-time large HSA distribution, if you want to maximize your HSA balances, is to approach the provider to whom you owe the large amount to negotiate terms. Perhaps you can pay the large expense over a period of months rather than all at once, so you can build the monthly payments into your personal budget to preserve HSA balances. Once you make a distribution from an HSA, you cannot (except under unusual circumstances) replace the money without having the new funds count against your annual contribution limit.

Finally, preserving balances may prove a useful strategy *before retirement*. For example, if you lose your job and have little or no income for a period of time, you can pay your health insurance premiums tax-free from your HSA as long as you are collecting unemployment benefits or are eligible to continue group coverage by exercising your COBRA rights. And if you've saved receipts reflecting expenses that you could have reimbursed from your HSA but did not, you can pay for any other expenses tax-free from your HSA up to the amount of deferred reimbursement. These expenses are not limited in any way; they may include health insurance premiums, mortgage, car payments, utilities, or a child's or grandchild's tuition.

Your strategy of deferring reimbursement may pay dividends for unexpected interruptions in income (such as a layoff) or as part of a well-planned life strategy: Retire at age sixty-two, continue your health insurance for eighteen months through COBRA, then purchase coverage in the individual market for an additional eighteen months until you are eligible to enroll in Medicare. You can reimburse your health insurance premiums tax-free during the COBRA period, then use the deferred reimbursements to pay your individual health insurance premiums tax-free from your HSA.

All this requires meticulous record keeping over the years to guard against a tax audit when you withdraw the money in retirement. Some HSA trustees will help you keep track of your expenses and categories, convert receipts to electronic form, and even keep a running total of how much you can withdraw tax-free at any point in time. Keep in mind that the IRS may not accept electronic copies of receipts but require the actual paper receipt during an audit.

Advantages of this strategy:

- Any expenses you incur after you establish your HSA and pay out of pocket create a tax-free withdrawal opportunity for any purpose, for the rest of your life.
- You retain higher HSA balances to pay eligible expenses tax-free in retirement.
- At age sixty-five, you can make distributions from your HSA for non-eligible expenses on the same terms as distributions from your qualified retirement account.

- You are not bound to continue the strategy. You still retain the right, at any time and with any expense, to change your approach and reimburse a large eligible expense immediately or make tax-free distributions for eligible expenses that you incurred in the past (but after you established your HSA).
- You may need to draw on assets to pay for expenses prior to retirement if you experience an interruption in or reduction to income. You can make distributions from your HSA tax-free for certain eligible expenses and for all other non-eligible expenses up to the value of your deferred tax-free distributions.

Disadvantages of this strategy:

- You may end up paying more in taxes, in the unlikely event that you have more money in your HSA than needed for medical expenses and your effective tax rate in retirement is higher than during your working years. (Note: This disadvantage may be outweighed by your greater financial capacity to pay higher taxes on expenses incurred during your higher-income working years than to pay lower taxes in a period of your life when you have fixed assets to generate income.)
- This strategy involves additional recordkeeping. While you need to retain receipts to substantiate tax-free distributions for eligible expenses in case of an income tax return audit (generally three years), you must retain those same records for decades if you want to preserve your ability to defer reimbursement and make a lump-sum distribution for non-eligible expenses. Some individuals may become overwhelmed by this recordkeeping responsibility.

Strategy Number 3

Know All Expenses That Are HSA-Eligible

Be sure to maximize the tax advantages that your HSA offers. Whether you need to reimburse expenses now or can delay reimbursement until later, knowing what expenses are eligible can help you maximize the utility of your account.

Many of the HSA strategies described here emphasize the use of an HSA as a long-term tax savings vehicle. For many owners, this approach, followed over a period of years, will result in a much more secure retirement. The difficulty in following this approach is that it often requires forgoing tax-free distributions in the short-term.

Some accountholders are in a financial position to delay reimbursements, pay eligible expenses with personal funds, and preserve HSA balances for future tax-free reimbursements.

Other accountholders, however, do not have that luxury. If you do not, your best strategy may be to maximize your tax savings now.

Most readers are familiar with the concept of "Section 213(d) expenses" through their participation in a Health FSA program. Health FSAs generally reimburse all Section 213(d) expenses. Employers can narrow that list but rarely do. The list includes cost-sharing for expenses covered by a health plan, certain other services typically not covered by a health plan (acupuncture, hearing aids, orthotics, and certain forms of complementary medicine). The list also includes non-cosmetic dental and vision expenses and over-the-counter equipment and supplies. In addition, all drugs and medicine are still eligible for reimbursement, though participants must have a valid prescription or physician's letter of medical necessity to reimburse these items (including over-the-counter remedies) through a Health FSA.

The list of expenses eligible for tax-free reimbursement from an HSA is the same—and then some. Let's first discuss certain often overlooked expenses eligible for tax-free reimbursement through both a Health FSA and an HSA, then focus on some expenses that are eligible for tax-free reimbursement from an HSA, but not from a Health FSA.

Often overlooked eligible expenses

- **Travel for medical care**—This category includes mileage, parking and under certain conditions, airfare, hotel, and meals. The travel must be in connection with a qualifying service. Mileage and parking are straight-forward for patients visiting local providers. **A tip**: If you are undergoing regular visits, such as a regimen of physical therapy or series of allergy shots, consider choosing a practitioner near where you work. You can reimburse the travel costs associated with these visits—in effect reimbursing tax-free your commuting expenses during those days. In 2015, the standard medical mileage rate is $0.23 per mile. Reimbursing transportation and related expenses tax-free often becomes more complicated when you travel out of town. Accompanying your child for surgery at your insurer's center of excellence in another region of the country generally would constitute qualified travel, hotel and meal expenses. Visiting a family member in Florida in March and undergoing a routing dermatological screening is somewhat riskier—it almost surely will result in a Health FSA administrator's rejecting the claim, and it will likely be scrutinized in an audit of HSA expenses.

- **Travel to conferences**—If you, your spouse, or dependent child has a diagnosed medical condition, you may be able to reimburse travel and fees associated with attending an educational convention specific to that condition. Common examples might include a conference on modifying the behavior of a child with ADHD or on the autism spectrum or a conference on exercise and nutritional strategies for individuals diagnosed with multiple sclerosis. Again, as with much of medical travel as described above, some programs are riskier than others when it comes to reimbursement. An appropriate weekend conference two hundred miles from home probably is less risky than a week-long cruise with a daily two-hour educational program. It is best to receive legal or tax counsel if you plan to reimburse such expenses tax-free from your HSA.

- **Expenses to maintain health**—Expenses that you incur to maintain good health generally are not eligible for tax-free reimbursement through either account. These expenses include health clubs, vitamins, and massages. On the other hand, if your doctor prescribes these services for certain medical conditions, they may be eligible for tax-free reimbursement. Medically necessary services might include a health club with a regimen prescribed by a physician to counteract morbid obesity, low HDL cholesterol, osteoporosis, or lower-back issues; prenatal vitamins, vitamins for individuals suffering from malabsorption of natural vitamins as a result of gastric bypass surgery and calcium supplements for women with a diagnosis of osteoporosis; and therapeutic massage as an alternative to physical therapy to treat a muscle condition. You need to know the rules, and in many cases, you will not be able to reimburse those expenses tax-free. For example, if you are already a member of a gym, you cannot reimburse your gym membership fees tax-free, even if your doctor prescribes a regimen to address a particular condition. Know the rules, though, and you might receive a benefit that you otherwise might overlook.

- **Home and auto modification**—If you have a handicap that results in your modifying your vehicle or your home, the costs associated with those modifications may be eligible expenses. Be careful, though, as you can reimburse only the portion of expenses directly related to the handicap, and you cannot reimburse any portion that increases the value of the asset. For example, installing a ramp to replace the front stairs to accommodate an eligible individual who cannot use stairs or installing railings in a hallway or bathtub probably would qualify as an eligible expense. An in-ground pool installed so that a family member with multiple sclerosis can experience water therapy probably would not be fully eligible for tax-free reimbursement (though joining a health club to participate in physician-prescribed water therapy probably would qualify).

- **Vision correction surgery and orthodontia**—Health insurers generally do not cover LASIK and other vision correction surgery, and dental policies usually offer only limited orthodontia coverage (and sometimes no coverage for adults). Do not assume that these expenses are cosmetic (your vanity dictates that you do not want to be caught dead in glasses, and you want to straighten your teeth to attract a suitable mate). These services treat an existing condition and therefore generally are considered medical treatments rather than cosmetic procedures. Thus, they are generally eligible for tax-free reimbursement.

- **Over-the-counter drugs and medicine**—As part of the Affordable Care Act of 2010, Congress determined that over-the-counter drugs and medicine (except for insulin) are no longer eligible for tax-free reimbursement from a tax-free account unless the drug or medicine is prescribed by a state-certified prescriber. This provision hit Health FSAs participants particularly hard, as many of them went on an annual end-of-year shopping spree to spend their remaining funds on ibuprofen, cough syrup, and other home remedies rather than forfeit unused balances. It probably does not make sense to visit the doctor (particularly when the visit is subject to the deductible under an HSA-qualified plan) to receive a prescription for a bottle of ibuprofen or cough drops. On the other hand, if your seasonal allergy or GERD medicine is now sold over the counter, you might ask your doctor for a prescription the next time you have an office visit. And it might not hurt to have the doctor prescribe a pain reliever and cough medicine "as needed" to reimburse those expenses as well.

- **Over-the-counter equipment and supplies**—The change in over-the-counter laws effective January 1, 2011, applies to drugs and medicine only. You can still reimburse eligible equipment and supplies tax-free from your HSA. That's the good news. The bad news is that this category is not large. The most common eligible expenses include adhesive bandages, gauze pads, elastic bandage wraps (Ace bandages, as well as form-fitting ankle, knee and elbow pads), and wrist splints for conditions like carpal tunnel syndrome. Many other eligible items— C-PAP machines and supplies, crutches, wheelchairs—

are covered by insurance as durable medical equipment. Even in this case, any portion of these services not covered by insurance is eligible for tax-free distribution from your HSA.

Advantages of this strategy:

- You can maximize your ability for tax-free reimbursement of eligible items and services now and in the future by knowing what is allowable. Many people are spending on eligible items and do not know it.
- Especially in an estate situation—remember, you have up to a year after the death of an accountholder to make tax-free distributions for eligible expenses from the HSA—you may be able to gain some tax benefits by reimbursing expenses that you otherwise might not think of.

Disadvantages of this strategy:

- Any funds that you reimburse for these items and services are funds not available for growth of the balance and not available for distribution in retirement, when you may have more limited income.
- As with any tax deduction, the lower net cost of purchasing a good or service might tempt you to buy something that you otherwise would not value in the absence of tax advantages. You must be sure—in this and all other cases—that you are making the purchase because you value the good or service and the tax advantages are "icing on the cake." It makes no sense to buy something that you do not really need just to receive a tax benefit, as you will not have those funds available for necessary eligible expenses in the future.

Strategy Number 4

Transfer Balances from an IRA to an HSA

You are allowed to make a one-time transfer or rollover from an IRA to your HSA in your lifetime.

This approach may make sense in your situation, but it does have tax implications. As with Strategy 2, "Delay Reimbursement and Save Receipts," you need to balance the impact of immediate vs. future tax savings. This strategy makes the most sense when you have a need to pay a large medical bill and do not have enough money to fund your HSA with a new tax-free contribution but do have access to funds in an IRA and want to pay the bill with the IRA funds without incurring an early withdrawal penalty. If you have funds available to make additional tax-free HSA contributions, you increase your tax savings and preserve your IRA for future use.

Understanding the Rules

The rules on this one-time transfer (a direct transfer from the IRA trustee to the HSA trustee) or rollover (a withdrawal from your IRA deposited into your HSA within sixty days) are very precise. (To avoid confusion, I will refer to transfers, the preferred method, throughout this chapter.) First, the source of the transfer must be a traditional IRA or Roth IRA. You cannot make a transfer from a 401(k), 403(b), SEP, SIMPLE, or other qualified retirement plan. If you have funds in another type of account other than an IRA and want to pursue this strategy, you can do so as long as the law allows you to transfer funds from that qualified retirement account to an IRA. For example, if you have a 401(k) or 403(b) balance that you kept in a former employer's plan, you can transfer a portion or all of those balances to an IRA, and then make a one-time transfer from that IRA to your HSA.

Second, the source of the transfer must be a single IRA. If you want to transfer $5,000 and have three IRAs with balances of about $2,000 each, you need to transfer the balances of two of the IRAs into the third IRA, then transfer $5,000 from the third IRA into your HSA.

Third, the transfer counts against your annual contribution limit from all sources. Thus, in 2016, the maximum that you can transfer is $3,350 if you are covered by a self-only contract or $6,750 if your coverage is a family contract (plus an additional $1,000 if you are age fifty-five or older). These figures are reduced by contributions from any other sources, including your employer. Read below, though, to learn how a husband and wife can double their transfers.

Fourth, you are allowed to make only one transfer per lifetime. If you are covered on a family contract, for example, you cannot transfer $6,650 in 2015, then an additional $6,750 (the 2016 inflation-adjusted contribution limit) the following year, etc. The only exception to the one-time rule is if you make a transfer up to the self-only contract maximum, then change from a self-only to a family contract that same calendar year (for example, you marry or adopt). In that case, you can make a second transfer up to the statutory maximum annual contribution for a family contract (less contributions from other sources) that applies to that calendar year. This option is not available if, for example, you made your self-only transfer in a year prior to switching to a family contract or if you do not make the additional transfer by April 15 of the year following the change from self-only to family contract (with that transfer amount attributed to the calendar year in which the contract size changed).

The "Testing Period"

Those are the rules about the transfers themselves. They are not complicated, and they allow most HSA accountholders to make such a transfer at some point. Once your make the transfer, you have to satisfy one other requirement. You must remain HSA-eligible throughout the testing period, defined as the first full twelve months after you make the transfer. For example, if you transfer $6,000 on June 20, 2016, your testing period commences July 1, 2016, and ends June 30, 2017.

If you lose HSA eligibility during this period, your entire transfer is considered a non-qualified distribution from your retirement account. The entire transferred amount is included in your taxable income and you are assessed an additional 10% tax if your distribution is subject to penalty. You can, however, keep the funds in your HSA, where they grow tax-free and can be distributed tax-free for eligible expenses in the future.

Determining When to Make a Transfer

Now that you know the rules and want to make a one-time transfer, here are some important factors to weigh when considering *when* to make the distribution:

> ➤ *My coverage level (self-only or family) will change in the near future due to an event other than marriage.* If the change is from family to self-only and you anticipate self-only coverage in future years, make the transfer this calendar year, while you can still transfer up to the family contract maximum contribution. If you are moving from self-only to family, you have more flexibility—you can make the

contribution this year or in a future year and transfer up to the family maximum contribution.

➤ *My coverage level will change from self-only to family this year due to my marriage, and I've already transferred up to the self-only maximum contribution this year.* You can make an additional transfer up to the family maximum *this* year only. If you completed a transfer up to the self-only contribution limit during a previous year, you cannot make another transfer. If you have not made a transfer prior to your marriage, you can make one transfer contribution up to the family maximum contribution limit at any time after your marriage that you remain covered on a family contract.

➤ *My coverage level will change in the next few years.* Make the transfer during the calendar year that you are covered under a family contract. That way, you'll have the freedom to transfer up to the family contract maximum.

➤ *My taxable income will rise or fall substantially next year.* Consider making the transfer in the year of lower taxable income. One of the few disadvantages of making a transfer is that you lose the tax advantages associated with contributions during that year (since each dollar transferred reduces your contributions—and thus reductions in taxable income—by $1,000 for that year). The value of the tax reduction is greater in years when you are subject to higher marginal tax rates.

➤ *I do not have an IRA.* At first glance, this situation seems simple. You cannot transfer any funds from an account that does not exist. Determine whether you have another type of retirement account that you can convert to an IRA. If not, keep this strategy in the back of your mind in case you find yourself with an account that you can convert to an IRA in the future (for example, when you leave your employer and have the option to convert your 401(k) or 403(b) to an IRA).

WHICH TYPE OF IRA IS THE BETTER SOURCE OF TRANSFER FUNDS?

As mentioned above, your transfer contribution can come from either a traditional IRA or a Roth IRA.

Traditional IRAs were created by ERISA, the landmark 1974 federal law governing retirement programs and self-insured health insurance plans. An IRA is a trust account that an eligible individual can establish to save for retirement. IRA balances grow tax-free. Distributions from traditional IRAs are included in taxable income. Accountholders are subject to penalties (beyond having taxes applied) if they make certain distributions before they are eligible (generally at age fifty-nine and a half) and if they do not begin to make mandatory distributions by a certain age (usually seventy and a half).

Contributions to a traditional IRA are often tax-deductible if the accountholder is not covered by an employer-sponsored retirement plan and has taxable income below a certain level. The tax deduction is phased out based on income.

Roth IRAs, named for their champion, the late former Sen. William V. Roth (R-Del.) were born as a result of tax reform in 1997. Roth IRA accountholders contribute after-tax dollars. Their balances grow tax-free and distributions are tax-free (except for premature withdrawals), with no required mandatory withdrawals at any age.

	Traditional IRA	Roth IRA
Contributions	Often tax-deductible	Not tax-deductible
Account growth	Tax-deferred	Tax-deferred
Distributions	Taxable income	Tax-free
Mandatory distributions?	Yes	No

So which account—traditional or Roth—is the better trust from which to transfer funds to an HSA? The clear choice in nearly all cases is the traditional IRA. In many cases, contributions to a traditional IRA are tax-deductible, which matches the tax treatment of HSA contributions. Balances grow tax-deferred in both accounts. Thus, so far in the analysis, there's no advantage to executing the transfer.

Traditional IRA distributions are always included in taxable income. You cannot make distributions for any expenses (with a few exceptions) without penalty and all distributions (with a few exceptions) are included in taxable income even after you are entitled to make distributions without penalty. You also must begin a schedule of mandatory contributions at a certain age, whether or not you actually need the money.

By contrast, HSA contributions for eligible expenses are always tax-free, regardless of your age or the amount of time since you established your HSA. You are not required to make mandatory distributions at any age; you can continue to build your balances forever and pass those balances to heirs, who do not have to make mandatory distributions at any age.

Think of it this way: You contribute $100 to your traditional IRA. Let's assume the contribution is tax-deductible. Over time, your contribution increases in value to $200 through tax-deferred growth. In retirement, you withdraw the $200. You pay perhaps $50 in taxes, reducing your spendable amount to $150.

By contrast, you contribute $100 to your HSA. This contribution is always tax-free. Your $100 increases to $200 with tax-deferred account growth. In retirement, you withdraw the same $200. If you spend the distribution on eligible medical, dental, and vision expenses, you can spend the full $200. If you spend it on other items not eligible for tax-free HSA distributions, you have the same $150 that you had with your IRA distribution.

So if you transfer funds from a traditional IRA to an HSA, the rollover consists of funds that (in most cases) had the same tax treatment for contributions and growth. Distributions from the HSA at age sixty-five are always treated at least as favorably as (and usually more favorably than) traditional IRA distributions.

	Keep in traditional IRA	Roll over to HSA
Contribution	$100	
Rollover to an HSA		$100
Account growth	$100	$100
Distribution	$200	$200
Taxes	$50	$0
Net distribution	$150	$200

While the funds are more effective in the HSA, you are still better off funding your HSA with new money in order to get an additional tax deduction, if you have the funds available.

If you roll over a balance from a Roth IRA, the scenario changes. With a Roth IRA, you contribute with post-tax dollars. You pay the taxes up front to enjoy the opportunity to make tax-free distributions for any expense. If you subsequently roll over that money to an HSA, you lose out under any scenario, unless you are strapped for cash to pay a large current medical bill:

> ➤ *You make distributions for eligible expenses:* You pay no taxes or penalties on these HSA distributions, but you would not have paid any taxes or penalties if you'd kept the money in your Roth IRA and made the same distributions. Meanwhile, in the year that you executed the transfer, you could not reduce your taxable income (HSA contributions) up to the amount of the transfer. You in effect paid taxes on the transferred funds twice—once when you placed the money in the Roth IRA, and again in the form of HSA pre-tax payroll contributions that

you had to forgo the year of the transfer. You would have been better off keeping your money in your Roth IRA and making a tax-free contribution to your HSA in the year of your Roth IRA transfer.

> *You make distributions for non-eligible expenses:* All distributions from the Roth IRA are tax-free, while HSA distributions for non-eligible expenses are taxable (and subject to a 20% penalty if you are not yet age sixty-five or disabled). In this scenario, you pay taxes on the contributions to your Roth IRA, your contributions grow tax-free whether in the Roth IRA or HSA and then your distribution is taxed. You would have been better off keeping the money in your Roth IRA and making a tax-free contribution to your HSA in the year of your Roth IRA transfer.

A Roth IRA provides a level of distribution flexibility that the HSA lacks since all distributions (subject to certain mild restrictions about the age of the Roth IRA) are tax-free. You pay for that flexibility by making post-tax contributions. Your HSA contributions are tax-free, but you face restrictions around distributions for non-eligible expenses. In a world of uncertainty as to when and for what purpose you may make future distributions, you are better off keeping Roth IRA funds where they are.

An important note on the transfer strategy: *Be disciplined!* You will not spend funds in your traditional or Roth IRAs because you've set them aside in a vehicle designed for retirement. If you move that money into an HSA, you've placed a retirement asset into an account that can reimburse today's expenses tax-free. To bolster this use, an HSA typically includes a debit card and at least one other form of easy withdrawals (paper checks or electronic bill pay). If your intent is to retain the transferred funds to grow in your HSA, you must resist the temptation to spend those funds on current eligible expenses and thus reduce your asset base.

Families Can Double
Their Transfers

Traditional and nontraditional families can adopt strategies to double their HSA transfer amounts when more than one adult on the health insurance contract is HSA-eligible. Here's how:

Husband and wife. Since both HSAs and IRAs are individual accounts (owned by only one person), a husband can complete a transfer valued up to the family HSA contribution maximum from his IRA to his HSA in one year, and his wife, if she's HSA-eligible, can make the same level of contribution to her HSA in a subsequent year.

Here's an example: The husband, who is the health plan subscriber, opens his HSA in 2015, when the maximum contribution for a family contract is $6,650. His employer gives him a $500 contribution every year. He can transfer the remaining $6,150 from his IRA to his HSA. He should consider completing the transfer early in the year so that he begins and ends his "testing period" sooner. In 2016, the husband receives another $500 employer contribution to his HSA. In 2016, the family maximum contribution increases to $6,750. His wife, if she's HSA-eligible, can open her own HSA and roll over up to $6,250 from her IRA to her HSA. Again, she should consider doing so early in the year to get past the twelve-month "testing period" sooner.

Because the family maximum contribution applies to traditional families (husband and wife), spouses can maximize total family rollovers only by having each spouse make a transfer in different years.

Non-spouses. The family maximum contributions may not apply (see Appendix B for a more complete discussion) to other situations in which two adults are covered on the same contract. These scenarios include domestic partners of the same or opposite sex, ex-spouses, separated spouses with a court-approved agreement of separate maintenance in place and adult children who are no longer their parents', or parent's tax dependent but remain on the family health insurance until their twenty-sixth birthday.

In these cases, HSA-eligible individuals can follow the same process outlined for husband and wife. The only difference is that all individuals covered on the health insurance contract can (probably) execute a transfer in the same year since the HSA contribution limits for husband and wife do not apply.

An important point to remember in these transfers (husband and wife, as well as non-spouse) is that IRAs and HSAs are individual accounts. There is no such thing as the "Addams Family IRA" or the "Brady Bunch HSA." Each party who wants to complete a transfer from an IRA to an HSA must have an IRA and an HSA in his or her name. One individual cannot transfer money from his IRA to another person's HSA, and two individuals with separate IRAs cannot execute transfer into a single HSA owned by one of them.

Advantages of an IRA-to-HSA Rollover:

- You can move funds from an account whose distributions are subject to ordinary income tax (IRA) to an account whose distributions are tax-free for eligible expenses. This can be very helpful if you have a large medical bill due and no current funds to contribute to your HSA to cover it. It is also possible that the transfer, coupled with years of compounded growth, can result in your saving thousands of dollars in taxes upon distribution.

Disadvantages of an IRA-to-HSA Rollover:

- Because the transfer counts against your annual contribution limit, a transfer limits your ability to reduce your taxable income in the year of the transfer. This disadvantage is not insignificant, and you must weigh carefully whether and when to pursue a transfer.

- If you execute a transfer and then promptly spend your transfer balances on HSA-eligible expenses, you receive the benefit of tax-free distributions, but you spend an asset. Many financial advisors would counsel against "eating the seed" by sacrificing balances in an asset that can generate additional tax-free income over time. See Strategy 6 for a simple solution to inadvertently spending down your asset.

Strategy Number 5

Divert Qualified Retirement Plan Contributions to Your HSA

You can position your HSA as an extension of your retirement funding strategy.

When you think about and manage your HSA as another retirement asset, you can become very creative in funding your HSA. Let's say you want to maximize your HSA contribution in a given year to save money for eligible expenses in retirement, but you do not have enough disposable income to contribute up to the HSA maximum for your contract type. Let's also say you are a diligent retirement saver and automatically defer 11% of your salary into your employer's 401(k) plan. Using the same money, you can reduce your taxes in retirement by allocating the savings differently in any given year.

Think about the following goals in deciding how to maximize savings and utility of 401-k and HSA dollars:

- First, take full advantage of the dollars your employer will contribute on your behalf such as matching 401-k contributions or employer contributions to the HSA.
- Next, make sure you cover your expected current medical expenditures from your HSA.

- Then, maximize your HSA contribution since it has superior flexibility.
- Finally, maximize your 401-k or other tax advantaged contributions.

Here's a scenario if you're under age fifty-five in 2016 (no "catch-up" contribution):

- You sign up for an HSA-qualified plan. Your employer offers a $1,500 employer contribution, and you'll save $1,000 in annual premiums by choosing the HSA-qualified plan rather than your employer's other option.
- You can contribute up to $6,750 (family contract maximum) into your HSA.
- You anticipate needing $3,550 in HSA funds to reimburse your 2016 eligible expenses, leaving you with a $3,000 HSA balance at the end of 2014.
- You earn $60,000 and defer 11% ($6,600) to your employer's 401(k) plan. The employer provides a 50% match on the first 6% of your salary that you defer.

Funding your HSA for your anticipated 2016 expenses: You need to fund your HSA to reimburse $3,550 of anticipated expenses. Your employer's $1,500 contribution and your $1,000 premium savings cover $2,500 of the total, leaving you with an additional $1,050 to find in your budget. That's an additional $87.50 per month gross, which will reduce your after-tax paycheck by about $60 per month. You need to find a way to save $60 per month to pay your medical, dental and vision expenses. Let's say $1,200 of those expenses are dental and vision and you pay $800 in prescription drug copays. That's $2,000 in expenses that you'll be paying with pre-tax dollars, which will save you $500 in taxes. You've just "funded" half the $1,050 gap with tax savings, leaving you with only $550 (less than $30 per month in reduced after-tax spending power) to find. If you find a way to contribute 14% of your salary to your 401(k), you'll get creative enough to find a way to live on $30 less in your monthly paycheck.

Channeling a portion of your retirement salary deferrals into your HSA: Now, let's figure out how to fund the other $3,000 of your HSA to save for future eligible expenses. You contribute $6,600 annually, or $550 monthly, to your 401(k). Your employer matches 50% of the first 6% of your salary that you contribute. So to maximize your employer's matching contribution (which you always want to do—it is free money, and in this case, it represents an automatic 50% return on your money as soon as you contribute), you must contribute at least $300 per month to your 401(k). That leaves an additional $250 of retirement savings to allocate between your 401(k) and your HSA.

If you take that $250 and contribute all of it to your HSA, you'll contribute an additional $3,000 annually, which is precisely your target.

After all is said and done, here's what your 2016 retirement savings looks like under the two scenarios—contributing 11% of your income to your 401(k) or allocating the same 11% between your 401(k) and your HSA:

	401(k) only	401(k) and HSA
Salary	$60,000	$60,000
11% retirement	$6,600	$6,600
401(k) contribution	$6,600	$3,600
Employer match	$1,800	$1,800
HSA contribution	$0	$3,000
Total 2014 contribution to "retirement" plans	$8,400	$8,400

At first glance, it looks like a wash. Either way, you contribute $8,400 to your retirement savings. So what's the difference? The difference is in the distributions. Let's fast-forward decades to retirement. You have a $3,000 medical bill that you have to pay from a retirement account. If you pay the bill from the 401(k), you'll have to withdraw $4,000 and pay taxes of $1,000 to net the $3,000 of after-tax dollars that you need to pay the bill. By contrast, you'll have to withdraw only $3,000 from your HSA since HSA distributions for eligible expenses are tax free.

How much do you want to deplete your assets to pay a $3,000 medical bill in retirement? $3,000 or $4,000? Answer that question correctly, and you can appreciate the long-term impact of making retirement funding decisions today.

Let's take it to the extreme. As you learned in Strategy 2, Fidelity estimates that a couple retiring today at age 65 will need approximately $220,000 to cover out-of-pocket health-related expenses in retirement. Would you rather withdraw $293,333 from a 401(k) to net $220,000 after taxes to pay your out-of-pocket retirement medical expenses, or withdraw $220,000 from your HSA? That's a difference of $73,333, which is money that you can continue to invest to increase your annual income in retirement (a very important consideration if inflation increases in the future) or leave to your heirs or the charitable organizations that mean the most to you.

Advantages of reallocating retirement savings:

- You can change your retirement standard of living dramatically with successful allocation strategies during your working years.
- These allocations have no impact on your take-home pay, so you are not sacrificing your current lifestyle for your future standard of living.

Disadvantages of reallocating retirement savings:

- It requires discipline not to spend the asset before retirement (but see Strategy 6 for a strategy to protect yourself against this temptation).
- It takes a little extra thinking every year. That extra hour of annual thinking, though, multiplied by twenty years results in the $73,333 savings illustrated above. That's the equivalent of earning nearly $4,000 per hour of thinking. Very few people in the world make $4,000 per hour of mental labor.

Strategy Number 6

Maintain Multiple HSAs

Most accountholders gain no advantage from owning multiple HSAs, but for some it is required and for others it can be a prudent optional strategy.

Maintaining and managing multiple HSAs usually does not increase total family HSA contributions or increase the number of individuals whose eligible expenses can be reimbursed tax-free from an HSA. There are, of course, exceptions, as you've learned already. Multiple HSAs in one family make sense for spousal catch-up contributions, in nontraditional/non-recognized relationships and with non-dependent adult children remaining on the family health plan to age twenty-six.

Even these exceptions to the general rule do not apply when one family member maintains more than one HSA. If your goal is to simplify your life as much as possible without missing any opportunities and to limit duplicate expenses, you typically would not consider owning two HSAs. A second HSA in most cases does not give you any privileges or opportunities that a single account does not offer.

However, under certain circumstances, it makes sense for you to own and manage two HSAs. The multiple-HSA scenario may help you execute the first three strategies more effectively. In each case, your goal is to build assets in your HSA, either by consciously transferring balances between HSAs, transferring funds from another asset (an IRA) to your HSA, or reallocating current retirement contributions between tax-advantaged accounts. A disadvantage to each of these strategies is that you must have the discipline not to spend money that you want to preserve as an asset when you deposit the funds into an HSA, with its easy access to distributions.

Think about it like this: You are planning a family vacation a year from now. It will cost $4,800, which means that you have to save $400 per month to reach your goal. Would you feel more confident in your ability to reach your target if you (1) kept the money in your checking account but committed not to spend it or (2) systematically moved $400 each month from your checking account into your savings account (or had $400 per month deducted from your paycheck or checking account directly into the savings account)?

You are much more likely to reach your $4,800 target using the latter approach, for three reasons.

First, when the funds are "out of sight, out of mind," you are not tempted to "borrow" $100 here or $75 there with the promise that you'll pay it back next month. If you are like most people, the type of financial situation that leads you to borrow one month will appear the next month as well.

Second, if you place the funds in the right type of account, you will not have easy access to the money. You will not be able to write a check because it is a savings account. If you do not request a debit card, you are further limited in your ability to make distributions. If the account is an online account or at a bank across town, you'll have a difficult time accessing the funds even if you are tempted.

And third, you'll receive a psychological boost every time you look at your savings account statement and see your account balance move closer to your financial goal.

The same holds true for an HSA. There are no designated "checking" or "saving" HSAs in the tax code. You might want to use a portion of your HSA contributions for immediate reimbursement (using the HSA like a Health FSA) while you preserve another portion (particularly when you've allocated those funds from an actual asset) for future tax-free distributions (using the HSA like an IRA). In this case, you might want to maintain two separate HSAs that you designate as your "spending" and "saving" HSAs.

The terms "spending" and "saving" have no legal meaning. Your trust agreements for your two HSAs will not be written any differently as a result of your strategy. Both accounts will offer you all the benefits of a standard HSA. The difference is in how you choose to utilize these two accounts.

A critical part of this strategy involves moving the money from one account to the other if you accept employer contributions or make pre-tax payroll contributions through your employer's Cafeteria Plan. Employers can (and usually do) limit their interaction to one HSA trustee. All employees who want to receive employer contributions or make pre-tax payroll allocations often must receive those funds in an HSA managed by the employer's preferred trustee. And it is important to make pre-tax payroll contributions through a Cafeteria Plan whenever possible since it is the only way for you (and your employer) to avoid payroll taxes.

You are allowed to make an unlimited number of trustee-to-trustee transfers. So it is possible to take a portion of your payroll deductions into your "spending" HSA and move them into your "saving" HSA or vice versa. Some trustees charge a fee (typically $25) to send money to another trustee, which makes this strategy very expensive to do monthly ($300) or even quarterly ($100). And if you choose a less frequent schedule to save money, and your payroll contributions go into the "spending" HSA, you may find yourself tempted to spend some of the money earmarked for "saving."

Here are some tips to guide you:

- If you are not making pre-tax payroll contributions, you do not have a problem. Just contribute after-tax dollars to each of the two accounts as you wish (you'll deduct all contributions when you file your personal income tax return for that year).

- You might want to look for a trustee that charges no fee or a lower fee to move money to your account with another HSA trustee, or a trustee that allows you to open a second HSA with that trustee and make transfers at no cost.

- You might want to see whether an HSA trustee allows you to link a personal savings or checking account directly to your HSA. In that case, you can link the number of your "saving" HSA to your "spending HSA" and make regular transfers yourself at no cost. Alternatively, a "spending" HSA with a checkbook (not all HSAs offer this feature) may allow you to accomplish the same result. Be sure to contact the "saving" HSA trustee to instruct it to label the incoming funds as a transfer (and with the "spending" HSA trustee after the fact to see whether it will classify those distributions as transfers). Otherwise, it will assume that the money represents a contribution, and your "spending" and "saving" HSA trustees will each report the same money to the IRS as contributions. Thus, if you contribute $6,750 in 2016 to your "spending" HSA and move $3,000 to your "saving" HSA, the two trustees' Form 5498 annual reports to the IRS will show a total of $9,750 in contributions. You'll face a compliance issue that you'll have to correct or suffer penalties and ongoing reporting requirements.

- Make sure you limit your access to the "saving" HSA balances. You might want to cut up the debit card and either put the checkbook away (in your safe deposit box, for example) or cut up the checkbook too and force yourself to apply to the trustee for a manual reimbursement check if you do need to access your "saving" HSA funds for an emergency.

- Look for an HSA with low transaction fees for your "spending" HSA. You'll use it like a Health FSA to reimburse current expenses. It will not have a high balance. Be sure that the account has no (or minimal) fees for using the debit card or checkbook. Look for an account with a low (or no) monthly maintenance fee. Do not choose an account with a higher monthly fee that is waived with a specific balance, as you may not have a balance high enough to waive fees in most months. And do not worry about interest rates or investment options—you will not have enough money in the account to build your balance via interest or to invest.

- Look for an HSA with the potential for account growth for your "saving" account (such as higher or tiered interest rates and a wide range of investment options). Do not worry about minimum balances to begin to invest—you'll maintain a large balance in the account. An account with a high monthly fee that's waived with a certain balance is okay since you'll maintain a large balance. Make sure, though, that the fees are waived with a certain balance so that you are not paying a monthly fee of $5 ($60 annually) even when you have a balance of $5,000 or more. You do not need debit card and checkbook access to your funds, since you are saving these balances long-term and do not want easy access to your money.

Advantages of this strategy:

- You sequester your funds into separate HSAs according to your intended use of the money, which limits your spending HSA balances intended for savings, either consciously or inadvertently. This advantage is a key to saving long-term in an HSA with high interest rates or excellent investment options without worrying about your level of discipline not to spend funds intended for savings.

Disadvantages of this strategy:

- You must manage multiple HSAs and may incur multiple administration fees (though the "saving" HSA should have fees waived at a certain balance level that you'll reach quickly).
- You must initiate periodic trustee-to-trustee transfers by whatever means make the most sense financially and in terms of compliance with IRS regulations and reporting requirements. You must be diligent to make sure all transferred money is coded correctly to avoid double counting tax-free contributions.

Strategy Number 7

Continue to Manage Your HSA When You Are No Longer HSA-Eligible

Your HSA life can be broken down into three or four distinct periods.

The first is the period of time during which you are HSA-eligible and thus can contribute to your HSA. The second is the time during which you are not eligible to contribute to your HSA due to a temporary event (you experience a gap between periods of coverage under an HSA-qualified plan, or, less typically, you access non-preventative, non-service-connected services through the VA or Indian Health Services).

Some accountholders may experience a third distinct period—the time during which they are not HSA-eligible, but may regain eligibility at some point before they lose eligibility for good. A common example is an HSA-eligible individual who changes jobs and enrolls in her new employer's group health insurance plan, which is not an HSA-qualified plan. She cannot make additional contributions, but at some point, she may change jobs again, or her new employer may change health plans, so that she's once again HSA-eligible.

The final period is when your are covered by Medicare and can no longer contribute but can only spend or pass your unused HSA dollars to your spouse or heirs.

The focus of this chapter is how to deal with the second and third situations. Let's start with temporarily not being HSA-eligible. The definition of this period is broad, essentially any period between when you were HSA-eligible and a permanent event like enrollment in Medicare. You may or may not eventually regain eligibility, and you may have no intention of ever regaining HSA eligibility, but we refer to this period as temporary because there remains a possibility that you could become HSA-eligible again.

When you are temporarily not HSA-eligible, your actions and strategies may have a huge impact on your ability to enjoy additional tax savings.

Let's look at an example. You establish an HSA effective April 1, 2006, and remain HSA-eligible until you leave your employer and enroll in your new employer's non-HSA-compliant health plan effective April 5, 2009. Then you switch jobs again and enroll in an HSA-qualified plan effective April 24, 2016. You thus have a seven-year period between May 1, 2009, and April 30, 2016, when you were not HSA-eligible.

As you've learned previously, once you establish an HSA, you can reimburse eligible expenses from that day forward for the rest of your life, provided that you retain an HSA balance. The phrase "provided that you retain an HSA balance" is the key to this strategy. As long as you have a positive balance in your HSA within eighteen months of your becoming HSA-eligible again, you can reimburse tax-free any eligible expenses that you (and your spouse and tax dependents at the time of the service) incur during any gaps in HSA eligibility (Internal Revenue Bulletin—Notice 2008-59, Question 41).

In our example above, as long as your HSA had a positive balance as of November 1, 2014 (eighteen months before you regained HSA eligibility as of May 1, 2016), you can reimburse any expenses that you incurred during the seven years between your loss of eligibility. Consider, though, that you often do not know whether or when you'll become HSA-eligible again, so it does not make sense to spend your entire balance and start the eighteen-month clock ticking if you are not certain that you'll regain eligibility in time.

You need to wait to become HSA-eligible again to replenish your old HSA (or a new HSA) with new contributions to reimburse those expenses, but you do not lose your ability to reimburse the expenses tax-free retroactively. As long as you have a positive balance within eighteen months of establishing the new HSA, your HSA establishment date reverts to the date that you established your original HSA.

By contrast, if your HSA balance dips to zero at any time within eighteen months prior to May 1, 2016 (November 1, 2014 or earlier), you can't reimburse any eligible expenses tax-free that you incurred since you depleted your old HSA balance with your new HSA money. When you establish your new HSA on or after May 1, 2016, you can use balances that you contribute to make tax-free distributions only for eligible expenses that you incur after the establishment date of the new HSA. Even if you make an immediate lump-sum contribution to the new HSA sufficient to reimburse some of the old expenses, the door to tax-free distributions for those eligible expenses has been slammed shut.

If you are a saver, you will not have a problem. On the other hand, if you used your HSA more like a Health FSA, without intentionally saving balances for future use, you may not have had a large balance when you lost your HSA eligibility as of May 1, 2009 in our example above. You may have begun to deplete the balance shortly thereafter, confident that you'd be HSA-eligible again soon and could start contributing and using new balances to reimburse expenses tax-free again. Time passed, you remained at the job without the HSA-qualified plan, and your

HSA balance dwindled. You stopped reimbursing any expenses because you were aware of this provision in the law.

However, your balance was sufficiently low that your HSA trustee began to deduct a $4 monthly administrative fee from the account. You offered to pay the admin fee with personal funds to preserve the HSA balance, but your trustee was not set up to collect admin fees outside the HSA. You thought about changing jobs just to regain HSA eligibility, but that move would have had consequences that outweighed the HSA advantage. You lost the account continuity that would have allowed you to keep your original HSA eligibility date.

Now that you understand the rule and how it applies to your ability to reimburse eligible expenses tax-free retroactively once you open your new HSA, here are some practical tips to help you manage a temporary HSA eligibility gap:

- Prepare for this situation beforehand by placing a portion of your HSA balance into a no-fee HSA. That way, with no deductions for monthly administrative fees, you'll retain a positive balance no matter how long your gap. Just commit not to spend the entire balance, no matter what. In this regard, it may be easier to keep a $50 balance in the new account than to keep $2,000. If you keep $50, it is not going to do much for you financially ($12.50 taxes saved) to spend it on a reimbursement during the eligibility gap. On the other hand, if you have a $2,000 balance, using that money for reimbursements will make a difference, and you may inadvertently spend the entire balance.
- Once you are in the eligibility gap and your balances are dwindling, look for a no-fee HSA for the same reasons listed above.
- If you cannot find a no-fee HSA, look for a trustee that will allow you to pay monthly administration fees with

personal funds so that you can retain what little balance remains in your HSA indefinitely, regardless of the monthly fees. You might want to pay six months' admin fees with personal funds, then pay each month or quarter thereafter so that you are always ahead in case you miss a payment, particularly if the trustee automatically pulls admin fees from the account balance if your payment is late. Some HSA trustees will bill annually for the fee outside the account to make it easier on savers in this situation.

Advantage of maintaining a balance during an HSA eligibility gap:

- You retain your ability to retroactively reimburse tax-free any expenses that you incur during the gap, even if you do not have sufficient HSA balances to reimburse until you are HSA-eligible again.

Disadvantage of maintaining a balance during an HSA eligibility gap:

- None. It requires some thinking and perhaps some action, but the benefit far outweighs the mental and perhaps time investment.

Strategy Number 8

Open an HSA with Self-Directed Investment Options

Note: Self-directed HSAs are particularly tricky, and you should proceed only with a high degree of caution. In 2012, two large self-directed IRA/HSA custodians faced lawsuits charging that the firms did not perform due diligence on investment managers with whom they do business and converted customers' funds for improper use, conspiracy, fraud, negligence and elder abuse, among other charges. If you plan to use a self-directed HSA, you must understand the investment before you commit funds, and you must be sure not to give your custodian the power to choose investments on your behalf.

Very few individuals understand the concept of a self-directed IRA or HSA.

Let's focus on the IRA world initially, as it is more familiar to most readers and forms the basis for HSA investment opportunities.

IRAs are held in trust by banks or investment companies. If your IRA trustee is a bank, your investment options may be limited to a savings account (paying market interest, which as of the early 2014 hovered around 0.10% to 0.20%) or a CD paying perhaps 1.0% annually. The savings account approach keeps your funds liquid, which is not necessary unless you are near or in retirement, or you use the IRA as a holding account from which you move funds to an investment opportunity. The CD ties up your money for a period of time (typically 12 to 60 months), which usually is not an issue since an IRA is a long-term investment. These are typically your only savings options in your bank-based IRA because they are the only options that the bank offers on any of its accounts.

To many investors, a "self-directed" IRA is an account that they establish with a mutual fund company or brokerage. With this account, the IRA owner can self-direct investments by allocating his IRA balances to various mutual fund, stock, and bond investments offered by the trustee. This account introduces the IRA owner to a whole new range of investment options, with potentially greater rewards and downside risk than a bank's investments. The trustee offers only investments that are IRS-approved, so you do not enter into a prohibited investment that might require you to liquidate the HSA and expose the entire balances to the tax and penalty consequences of a premature distribution.

For many, a self directed HSA will simply open up the list of investments from a restricted set of twenty to thirty mutual funds to include individual stocks and bonds, options, and ETFs. Others go a bit further to allow gold and other commodities, etc.

A true self-directed IRA or HSA offers far more investment options than standard stocks, bonds, and mutual funds. With a true self-directed IRA, the trustee does not filter any investment options that may not meet IRS guidelines. You are responsible for knowing which investments are permitted. In exchange for this increased level of responsibility, you gain a wide range of investment options. Did you know, for example, that you can invest your IRA or HSA balances in the following investments?

- income-producing residential real estate

- commercial real estate, including office buildings and malls
- businesses
- private mortgages
- business loans

The tax code imposes some restrictions on your active involvement in these investments, and you cannot invest in these opportunities when certain relatives are involved. And there are certain investments that are not permitted at all, including insurance contracts and collectibles that gives you the opportunity to impress people when you display them. Non-permitted examples include art work, wine, baseball cards and coins.

Think about the possibilities to build the value of your IRA or HSA by investing in one of the following opportunities:

- A family from your church declared bankruptcy a year ago when the husband had to leave his job to care for his terminally ill wife. She subsequently passed away, and now he earns a high income again. With the bankruptcy on his record, though, he cannot qualify for an auto loan, and he has only $6,000 to put down on a $24,000 car. You can lend him the remaining $18,000 at 12% interest, and your HSA will be listed on the title as lienholder, which allows you to repossess the car and sell it for enough to restore your funds if he defaults.
- Your real estate agent friend tells you about a fixer-upper property on the outskirts of town. You approach the buyer and pay a $2,000 option on the property, with sixty days to complete the transfer or forfeit your option deposit. You know a contractor who rehabs houses. He sees the property, and you assign your option to him for $7,500.
- Your neighbor has a successful electrical contracting company. He needs to invest $45,000 in a new piece of

equipment. The bank will charge him 9% interest. You have funds in your HSA earning 1.5% interest, and you offer to extend a loan to him of $35,000 at 7% interest if he puts $10,000 down. The down payment minimizes your investment risk.

- Your husband's coworker invests in apartment buildings, rehabs them, and sells or holds them. She needs quick access to $50,000 to complete renovations on a building that she bought for $400,000. It is worth $500,000 before the renovations and an estimated $650,000 after-repair value. She'll pay you $75,000 when she sells or in a year, whichever comes first. Her equity more than covers the value of your loan.

Can you see the possibilities? Most people's HSA balances are not as high as their IRA balances because HSAs are newer, HSA annual contribution limits are much lower, they offer tax-free distributions at any age for eligible expenses, and individuals can roll over substantial 401(k) or 403(b) balances into IRAs when they leave their jobs. The first two scenarios above are realistic for HSA owners in one to four years, depending on how aggressively they save. The last two are more appropriate after a decade or so (or earlier, if they make a few astute smaller deals).

A self-directed HSA makes sense for some accountholders, especially those who have special knowledge in areas such as finance, business, real estate, and lending. And even if these true self-directed opportunities do not fall within your comfort sphere, you might want to at least branch out into HSAs that offer wide access to mutual funds, stocks, and bonds so that you have more opportunities to build your balances.

Here are some tips if you are considering self-directed HSAs (or if you are now interested in reevaluating your IRA investment strategy—the rules are the same):

- Examine costs carefully. Self-directed HSAs are often much more expensive than traditional HSAs. The costs may include an annual account maintenance fee and perhaps a variable fee based on a percentage of the value of the underlying investments. You want to be sure that you minimize costs while gaining access to the types of investments that you seek.

- Do not expect the trustee to provide a lot of advice and guidance. The self-directed trustee may help you find attorneys or accountants who are expert in your desired area of investment, but these services typically are at an additional cost to you. Your HSA trustee will not assume the risk of evaluating your potential investments for compliance with IRS regulations.

- If you venture beyond normal stocks, bonds, and mutual funds, you'll want to place each investment in a separate HSA. No matter how well you or your advisor knows the law, you may make an investment that the IRS later rules is a prohibited transaction. When that happens, the HSA is liquidated and the entire balance is considered a distribution for a non-eligible expense (thus included in taxable income and subject to a 20% penalty if applicable). You'll want to segregate each investment into a separate HSA so that if one investment is deemed a prohibited transaction, you need to liquidate only the HSA containing that investment rather than your entire HSA balance.

- Check your trustee's ability to move quickly. You may need to make an investment with no lead time. How quickly can the trustee move to create a new HSA to house a new investment and wire the money to the intended recipient? Speed may be more important than other account features, and it may make sense to pay a higher maintenance fee or higher fees per investment to be able to set up and fund an investment faster. To gain additional control over reaction time, you may consult with an attorney to set up a self-directed HSA that owns a Limited Liability Company, or LLC. You manage the LLC, which opens a checking account. You then have checkbook access to your HSA funds and can respond instantly to an opportunity. This strategy is advanced and poses additional compliance risks to the uninitiated, but sophisticated IRA investors know the value of this approach and use it while remaining in compliance with IRS regulations.

Advantages of self-directed HSAs

- You have an opportunity to increase your earnings dramatically, particularly in an era of very low interest rates and slow stock market growth.
- You can apply your knowledge of particular investments to pursue opportunities for which you otherwise may not have the personal funds.
- Because your HSA is a long-term account that you do not plan to liquidate until retirement, you can make a long-term investment commitment without impacting your current lifestyle.

Disadvantages of self-directed HSAs

- They are more expensive to open and maintain than traditional HSAs.
- They are riskier if you do not have appropriate legal, financial, and tax counsel. The trustee does not attempt to limit your investment activity to instruments that definitely comply with IRS regulations.

PART 4
APPENDICES

Appendix A

IRC Section 223—Health Savings Accounts

(a) Deduction allowed

In the case of an individual who is an eligible individual for any month during the taxable year, there shall be allowed as a deduction for the taxable year an amount equal to the aggregate amount paid in cash during such taxable year by or on behalf of such individual to a health savings account of such individual.

(b) Limitations

1. In general

The amount allowable as a deduction under subsection (a) to an individual for the taxable year shall not exceed the sum of the monthly limitations for months during such taxable year that the individual is an eligible individual.

2. Monthly limitation

The monthly limitation for any month is 1/12 of
    (A) in the case of an eligible individual who has self-only coverage under a high deductible health plan as of the first day of such month, $2,250.

(B) in the case of an eligible individual who has family coverage under a high deductible health plan as of the first day of such month, $4,500.

3. **Additional contributions for individuals fifty-five or older**

(A) In general

In the case of an individual who has attained age fifty-five before the close of the taxable year, the applicable limitation under subparagraphs (A) and (B) of paragraph (2) shall be increased by the additional contribution amount.

(B) Additional contribution amount

For purposes of this section, the additional contribution amount is the amount determined in accordance with the following table:

Taxable year	Additional contribution amount
2004	$ 500
2005	$ 600
2006	$ 700
2007	$ 800
2008	$ 900
2009 and thereafter	$1,000

4. **Coordination with other contributions**

The limitation which would (but for this paragraph) apply under this subsection to an individual for any taxable year shall be reduced (but not below zero) by the sum of—

(A) the aggregate amount paid for such taxable year to Archer MSAs of such individual,

(B) the aggregate amount contributed to health savings accounts of such individual which is excludable from the taxpayer's gross income for such taxable year under section 106(d) (and such amount shall not be allowed as a deduction under subsection (a)), and

(C) the aggregate amount contributed to health savings accounts of such individual for such taxable year under section 408(d)(9) (and such amount shall not be allowed as a deduction under subsection (a)).

Subparagraph (A) shall not apply with respect to any individual to whom paragraph (5) applies.

5. **Special rule for married individuals**

In the case of individuals who are married to each other, if either spouse has family coverage—

(A both spouses shall be treated as having only such family coverage (and if such spouses each have family coverage under different plans, as having the family coverage with the lowest annual deductible), and

(B) the limitation under paragraph (1) (after the application of subparagraph (A) and without regard to any additional contribution amount under paragraph (3))—

(i) shall be reduced by the aggregate amount paid to Archer MSAs of such spouses for the taxable year, and

(ii) after such reduction, shall be divided equally between them unless they agree on a different division.

6. **Denial of deduction to dependents**

No deduction shall be allowed under this section to any individual with respect to whom a deduction under section 151 is allowable to another taxpayer for a taxable year beginning in the calendar year in which such individual's taxable year begins.

7. Medicare eligible individuals

The limitation under this subsection for any month with respect to an individual shall be zero for the first month such individual is entitled to benefits under title XVIII of the Social Security Act and for each month thereafter.

8. Increase in limit for individuals becoming eligible individuals after the beginning of the year

(A) In general

For purposes of computing the limitation under paragraph (1) for any taxable year, an individual who is an eligible individual during the last month of such taxable year shall be treated—

(i) as having been an eligible individual during each of the months in such taxable year, and

(ii) as having been enrolled, during each of the months such individual is treated as an eligible individual solely by reason of clause (i), in the same high deductible health plan in which the individual was enrolled for the last month of such taxable year.

(B) Failure to maintain high deductible health plan coverage

(i) In general. If, at any time during the testing period, the individual is not an eligible individual, then—

(I) gross income of the individual for the taxable year in which occurs the first month in the testing period for which such individual is not an eligible individual is increased by the aggregate amount of all contributions to the health savings account of the individual which could not have been made but for subparagraph (A), and

(II) the tax imposed by this chapter for any taxable year on the individual shall be increased by 10 percent of the amount of such increase.

(ii) Exception for disability or death. Subclauses (I) and (II) of clause (i) shall not apply if the individual ceased to be an eligible individual by reason of the death of the individual or the individual becoming disabled (within the meaning of section 72(m)(7)).

(iii) Testing period. The term "testing period" means the period beginning with the last month of the taxable year referred to in subparagraph (A) and ending on the last day of the 12th month following such month.

(c) Definitions and special rules

For purposes of this section—

1. Eligible individual

(A) In general

The term "eligible individual" means, with respect to any month, any individual if –

(i) such individual is covered under a high deductible health plan as of the first day of such month, and

(ii) such individual is not, while covered under a high deductible health plan, covered under any health plan—

(I) which is not a high deductible health plan, and

(II) which provides coverage for any benefit which is covered under the high deductible health plan.

(B) Certain coverage disregarded

Subparagraph (A)(ii) shall be applied without regard to—

(I) coverage for any benefit provided by permitted insurance,

(ii) coverage (whether through insurance or otherwise) for accidents, disability, dental care, vision care, or long-term care, and

(iii) for taxable years beginning after December 31, 2006, coverage under a health flexible spending arrangement during any period immediately following the end of a plan year of such arrangement during which unused benefits or contributions remaining at the end of such plan year may be paid or reimbursed to plan participants for qualified benefit expenses incurred during such period if—

(I) the balance in such arrangement at the end of such plan year is zero, or

(II) the individual is making a qualified HSA distribution (as defined in section 106(e)) in an amount equal to the remaining balance in such arrangement as of the end of such plan year, in accordance with rules prescribed by the Secretary.

2. High deductible health plan

(A) In general

The term "high deductible health plan" means a health plan—

> (i) which has an annual deductible which is not less than—
>> (I) $1,000 for self-only coverage, and
>> (II) twice the dollar amount in subclause (I) for family coverage, and
> (ii) the sum of the annual deductible and the other annual out-of-pocket expenses required to be paid under the plan (other than for premiums) for covered benefits does not exceed—
>> (I) $5,000 for self-only coverage, and
>> (II) twice the dollar amount in subclause (I) for family coverage.

(A) Exclusion of certain plans

Such term does not include a health plan if substantially all of its coverage is coverage described in paragraph (1)(B).

(C) Safe harbor for absence of preventive care deductible

(B) A plan shall not fail to be treated as a high deductible health plan by reason of failing to have a deductible forSpecial rules for network plans

In the case of a plan using a network of providers—

> (i) Annual out-of-pocket limitation. Such plan shall not fail to be treated as a high deductible health plan by reason of having an out-of-pocket limitation for services provided outside of such network which exceeds the applicable limitation under subparagraph (A)(ii).
> (ii) Annual deductible. Such plan's annual deductible for services provided outside of such network shall not be taken into account for purposes of subsection (b)(2).

3. Permitted insurance

The term "permitted insurance" means—
    (A) insurance if substantially all of the coverage provided under such insurance relates to—
        (i) liabilities incurred under workers' compensation laws,
        (ii) tort liabilities,
        (iii) liabilities relating to ownership or use of property, or
        (iv) such other similar liabilities as the Secretary may specify by regulations,
    (B) insurance for a specified disease or illness, and
    (C) insurance paying a fixed amount per day (or other period) of hospitalization.

4. Family coverage

The term "family coverage" means any coverage other than self-only coverage.

5. Archer MSA

The term "Archer MSA" has the meaning given such term in section 220(d).
    (d) Health savings account
    For purposes of this section—

1. In general

The term "health savings account" means a trust created or organized in the United States as a health savings account exclusively for the purpose of paying the qualified medical expenses of the account beneficiary, but only if the written governing instrument creating the trust meets the following requirements:

(A) Except in the case of a rollover contribution described in subsection (f)(5) or section 220(f)(5), no contribution will be accepted—

(i) unless it is in cash, or

(ii) to the extent such contribution, when added to previous contributions to the trust for the calendar year, exceeds the sum of—

(I) the dollar amount in effect under subsection (b)(2)(B), and

(II) the dollar amount in effect under subsection (b)(3)(B).

(B The trustee is a bank (as defined in section 408(n)), an insurance company (as defined in section 816), or another person who demonstrates to the satisfaction of the Secretary that the manner in which such person will administer the trust will be consistent with the requirements of this section.

(C) No part of the trust assets will be invested in life insurance contracts.

(D) The assets of the trust will not be commingled with other property except in a common trust fund or common investment fund.

(E) The interest of an individual in the balance in his account is nonforfeitable.

2. Qualified medical expenses

(A) In general

The term "qualified medical expenses" means, with respect to an account beneficiary, amounts paid by such beneficiary for medical care (as defined in section 213(d) 1 for such individual, the spouse of such individual, and any dependent (as defined in section 152, determined without regard to subsections (b)(1), (b)(2), and (d)(1)(B) thereof) of such individual, but only to the extent such amounts are not compensated for by insurance or otherwise. Such term shall include an amount paid for medicine or a drug only if such medicine or drug is a prescribed drug (determined without regard to whether such drug is available without a prescription) or is insulin.

(B) Health insurance may not be purchased from account

Subparagraph (A) shall not apply to any payment for insurance.

(C) Exceptions

Subparagraph (B) shall not apply to any expense for coverage under—
  (i) a health plan during any period of continuation coverage required under any Federal law,
  (ii) a qualified long-term care insurance contract (as defined in section 7702B(b)),
  (iii) a health plan during a period in which the individual is receiving unemployment compensation under any Federal or State law, or
  (iv) in the case of an account beneficiary who has attained the age specified in section 1811 of the Social Security Act, any health insurance other than a medicare supplemental policy (as defined in section 1882 of the Social Security Act).

3. Account beneficiary

The term "account beneficiary" means the individual on whose behalf the health savings account was established.

4. Certain rules to apply

Rules similar to the following rules shall apply for purposes of this section:

(A) Section 219(d)(2) (relating to no deduction for rollovers).

(B) Section 219(f)(3) (relating to time when contributions deemed made).

(C) Except as provided in section 106(d), section 219(f)(5) (relating to employer payments).

(D) Section 408(g) (relating to community property laws).

(E) Section 408(h) (relating to custodial accounts).

(e) Tax treatment of accounts

1. In general

A health savings account is exempt from taxation under this subtitle unless such account has ceased to be a health savings account. Notwithstanding the preceding sentence, any such account is subject to the taxes imposed by section 511 (relating to imposition of tax on unrelated business income of charitable, etc. organizations).

2. Account terminations

Rules similar to the rules of paragraphs (2) and (4) of section 408(e) shall apply to health savings accounts, and any amount treated as distributed under such rules shall be treated as not used to pay qualified medical expenses.

(f) Tax treatment of distributions

1. Amounts used for qualified medical expenses

Any amount paid or distributed out of a health savings account which is used exclusively to pay qualified medical expenses of any account beneficiary shall not be includible in gross income.

2. Inclusion of amounts not used for qualified medical expenses

Any amount paid or distributed out of a health savings account which is not used exclusively to pay the qualified medical expenses of the account beneficiary shall be included in the gross income of such beneficiary.

3. Excess contributions returned before due date of return

(A) In general

If any excess contribution is contributed for a taxable year to any health savings account of an individual, paragraph (2) shall not apply to distributions from the health savings accounts of such individual (to the extent such distributions do not exceed the aggregate excess contributions to all such accounts of such individual for such year) if—

(i) such distribution is received by the individual on or before the last day prescribed by law (including extensions of time) for filing such individual's return for such taxable year, and

(ii) such distribution is accompanied by the amount of net income attributable to such excess contribution.

Any net income described in clause (ii) shall be included in the gross income of the individual for the taxable year in which it is received.

(B) Excess contribution

For purposes of subparagraph (A), the term "excess contribution" means any contribution (other than a rollover contribution described in paragraph (5) or section 220(f)(5)) which is neither excludable from gross income under section 106(d) nor deductible under this section.

4. **Additional tax on distributions not used for qualified medical expenses**

(A) In general

The tax imposed by this chapter on the account beneficiary for any taxable year in which there is a payment or distribution from a health savings account of such beneficiary which is includible in gross income under paragraph (2) shall be increased by 20% of the amount which is so includible.

(B) Exception for disability or death

Subparagraph (A) shall not apply if the payment or distribution is made after the account beneficiary becomes disabled within the meaning of section 72(m)(7) or dies. Exception for distributions after medicare eligibility Subparagraph (A) shall not apply to any payment or distribution after the date on which the account beneficiary attains the age specified in section 1811 of the Social Security Act.

5. **Rollover contribution**

An amount is described in this paragraph as a rollover contribution if it meets the requirements of subparagraphs (A) and (B).

(A) In general

Paragraph (2) shall not apply to any amount paid or distributed from a health savings account to the account beneficiary to the extent the amount received is paid into a health savings account for the benefit of such beneficiary not later the sixtieth day after the day on which the beneficiary receives the payment or distribution.

(B) Limitation
This paragraph shall not apply to any amount described in subparagraph (A) received by an individual from a health savings account if, at any time during the 1-year period ending on the day of such receipt, such individual received any other amount described in subparagraph (A) from a health savings account which was not includible in the individual's gross income because of the application of this paragraph.

6. **Coordination with medical expense deduction**

For purposes of determining the amount of the deduction under section 213, any payment or distribution out of a health savings account for qualified medical expenses shall not be treated as an expense paid for medical care.

7. **Transfer of account incident to divorce**

The transfer of an individual's interest in a health savings account to an individual's spouse or former spouse under a divorce or separation instrument described in subparagraph (A) of section 71(b)(2) shall not be considered a taxable transfer made by such individual notwithstanding any other provision of this subtitle, and such interest shall, after such transfer, be treated as a health savings account with respect to which such spouse is the account beneficiary.

8. **Treatment after death of account beneficiary**

(A) Treatment if designated beneficiary is spouse

If the account beneficiary's surviving spouse acquires such beneficiary's interest in a health savings account by reason of being the designated beneficiary of such account at the death of the account beneficiary, such health savings account shall be treated as if the spouse were the account beneficiary.

(B) Other cases

(i) In general. If, by reason of the death of the account beneficiary, any person acquires the account beneficiary's interest in a health savings account in a case to which subparagraph (A) does not apply—

(I) such account shall cease to be a health savings account as of the date of death, and

(II) an amount equal to the fair market value of the assets in such account on such date shall be includible if such person is not the estate of such beneficiary, in such person's gross income for the taxable year which includes such date, or if such person is the estate of such beneficiary, in such beneficiary's gross income for the last taxable year of such beneficiary.

(ii) Special rules

(I) Reduction of inclusion for predeath expenses. The amount includible in gross income under clause (i) by any person (other than the estate) shall be reduced by the amount of qualified medical expenses which were incurred by the decedent before the date of the decedent's death and paid by such person within 1 year after such date.

(II) Deduction for estate taxes. An appropriate deduction shall be allowed under section 691(c) to any person (other than the decedent or the decedent's spouse) with respect to amounts included in gross income under clause (i) by such person.

(g) Cost-of-living adjustment

1. In general

Each dollar amount in subsections (b)(2) and (c)(2)(A) shall be increased by an amount equal to—

(A) such dollar amount, multiplied by

(B) the cost-of-living adjustment determined under section 1(f)(3) for the calendar year in which such taxable year begins determined by substituting for "calendar year 1992" in subparagraph (B) thereof—

(i) except as provided in clause (ii), "calendar year 1997", and

(ii) in the case of each dollar amount in subsection (c)(2)(A), "calendar year 2003".

In the case of adjustments made for any taxable year beginning after 2007, section 1(f)(4) shall be applied for purposes of this paragraph by substituting "March 31" for "August 31", and the Secretary shall publish the adjusted amounts under subsections (b)(2) and (c)(2)(A) for taxable years beginning in any calendar year no later than June 1 of the preceding calendar year.

2. Rounding

If any increase under paragraph (1) is not a multiple of $50, such increase shall be rounded to the nearest multiple of $50.

(h) Reports

The Secretary may require—

(1) the trustee of a health savings account to make such reports regarding such account to the Secretary and to the account beneficiary with respect to contributions, distributions, the return of excess contributions, and such other matters as the Secretary determines appropriate, and

(2) any person who provides an individual with a high deductible health plan to make such reports to the Secretary and to the account beneficiary with respect to such plan as the Secretary determines appropriate. The reports required by this subsection shall be filed at such time and in such manner and furnished to such individuals at such time and in such manner as may be required by the Secretary.

Appendix B

Other HSA Resources

IRS Notices

IRS Notice 2004-2—Original HSA guidance

IRS Notice 2004-23—HSA safe harbor for preventive care

IRS Notice 2004-30—HSA HDHP and prescription drug plan interaction

IRS Rev. Rul. 2004-45—HSA interaction with FSAs and HRAs

IRS Notice 2004-50—First comprehensive HSA guidance

IRS Notice 2005-8—HSAs and certain business owners

IRS Notice 2005-86—HSAs and Health FSA grace period

IRS Notice 2007-22—Rollovers from FSAs and HRAs to HSAs

IRS Notice 2008-51—Rollovers from an IRA to an HSA

IRS Notice 2008-52—HOPE Act of 2006 changes to HSAs

IRS Notice 2008-59—Updated general HSA guidance

IRS Notice 2010-59—OTC drugs and reimbursement accounts

IRS Notice 2011-5—OTC item purchases with debit cards

IRS Notice 2012-14—HSAs and Indian Health Service coverage

DOCUMENTS PUBLISHED ANNUALLY

IRS Publication 969—Annual guide to tax law and reimbursement accounts

IRS Publication 502—Annual guide to expenses eligible for tax-favored reimbursement under the tax code

IRS Form 1099—Report of distributions from an HSA, sent by HSA trustee to IRS and accountholder by January 31

IRS Form 5329—Report of excess contributions filed with personal income tax return

IRS Form 5498—Report of contributions to an HSA and fair market value of the HRA at year's end, sent by HSA trustee to IRS and accountholder by May 31

IRS Form 8889—Report of account activity filed with personal income tax return

About the Author

Todd Berkley is a leading practitioner in managing the business of health savings accounts (HSA) and is now a leading consultant focused on CDH growth strategies. His firm, HSA Consulting Services, LLC., is focused on HSA growth and also runs AskMrHSA.com, America's #1 educational resource for health savings accounts.

As HSA business leader for OptumHealth Bank (part of UnitedHealthcare) from 2005 to 2012, he was a driving force from shortly after start-up to making Optum a perennial industry leader in health accounts.

While at Optum, Optum's HSA business grew from 50,000 accounts to over 850,000 with balances exceeding $1.7 billion. Todd drove many industry innovations, such as publishing insights into consumer spending saving and investing activities, allowing consumers to trade off pricing elements to meet their individual needs, and guiding the development of a best-in-class web experience and education suite.

Todd is a member of ABA HSA Council and has been an active member of AHIP HSA Leadership Council and ECFC Working Group and other industry advocacy activities. He was instrumental in helping the industry tell its story to key lawmakers, regulators, and administrators during the health reform debate, helping to preserve HSAs' growing impact in health care.

Todd's career in consumer banking and investment product management and sales spans four decades and includes key roles at Magna Bank (now Regions), Norwest (now Wells Fargo), US Bank, and Sit Investment Associates, in addition to Optum.

Todd received his undergraduate degree from McKendree College in Lebanon, Illinois. He earned his MBA at the Harvard Graduate School of Business and is a past president of the HBS Club of Minnesota.

A native of Omaha, Nebraska, Mr. Berkley and his family live in Minnetonka, Minnesota. Todd's family has been on an HSA plan since 2006 and owns more than twenty HSA accounts to keep a pulse on the latest developments at key HSA custodians.

45053796R00157

Made in the USA
Middletown, DE
23 June 2017